Muay Thai:

The Footwork

(Black and White Edition)

The Secret to Learning the Art of 8 Limbs

By Anthony J. Yuan

(Kru Tony)

Copyright © 2018 by Anthony J. Yuan

All rights reserved. No part of this publication may be reproduced, distributed or transmitted in any form or by any means, including photocopying, recording, or other electronic or mechanical methods, without the prior written permission of the publisher, except in the case of brief quotations embodied in critical reviews and certain other noncommercial uses permitted by copyright law.

Anthony J. Yuan

ayuan@mastermindmuaythai.com

ISBN: 9781980381334

TABLE OF CONTENTS

WHAT TO EXPECT FROM THIS BOOK 1

CHAPTER 1 – STARTING POINT – BREAKING DOWN THE MUAY THAI STANCE . 3

    The Two Fighting Angles 3

    The Feet Position for the Two Fighting Angles 4

    The Muay Thai Stance – Wide vs. Narrow 5

    The Stance – How to Do it 7

CHAPTER 2 - THE ART OF MUAY THAI FOOTWORK 10

    The Importance of Footwork in Muay Thai 10

    The 19 Footwork Movement Skills of Muay Thai 11

        1. Step Forward 12

        2. Retreat 13

        3. Switch Stance Forward 14

        4. Switch Stance Back 15

        5. 1/4 Turn Out (left) 17

        6. 1/4 Turn Out (right) 18

        7. Diagonal Retreat (left) 19

        8. Diagonal Retreat (right) 20

        9a. 1/8 Turn In (left) 22

        9b. 1/4 Turn In (left) 23

        10a. 1/8 Turn In (right) 24

        10b. 1/4 Turn In (right) 25

        11. Pivot Step (left) 26

        12. Pivot Step (right) 27

        13. Move Feet Around a Circle 29

        14. Slant Step (left) 32

15. Slant Step (right)...33

16. Zig-Zag Footwork..34

17. Parry Mid-line..36

18. Lift Knee..37

19. Three Position Stepping..39

CHAPTER 3 – WHAT IS MAE MAI MUAY THAI?..45

The Muay Thai Arsenal - At a Glance..46

CHAPTER 4 – THE ART OF USING FISTS..47

How to Make a Fist..47

3 Ways to Position Your Fists for Punching...48

Types of Punches..49

Straight Punches...50

    Jab..51

    Jumping Jab..52

    Cross...54

Curved Punches..56

    Hooks..56

    Uppercut...57

    Short Uppercut..58

    High Uppercut...60

    Short Overhand...61

    Long Overhand..62

Developing Hand and Foot Correlation for Punching................................63

    The Principle of 'Same Time'...63

CHAPTER 5 – THE ART OF USING FOOT...64

The Difference Between the Teep and The Kick 64

Kicks 65

    Straight Kick 65

    Diagonal Kick 67

    High Cut Kick 68

    Low Cut Kick 70

    Arcing Down Kick 71

    Spinning Back Kick 72

Teeps 73

    Straight Teep 74

    Side Teep 77

    Backward Teep 78

CHAPTER 6 – THE ART OF USING KNEES **79**

    Straight Knee 80

    Flare Knee 81

    Curve Knee 82

    Flying Knee 83

    Blocking Knee 83

CHAPTER 7 – THE ART OF USING ELBOWS **84**

    Downward Hit Elbow 85

    Cut Elbow 86

    Up Elbow 87

    Spear Elbow 89

    Tomahawk Elbow 90

    Reverse Elbow 92

CHAPTER 8 – THE LOSING CYCLE OF WEAPONS **94**

CHAPTER 9 – BASIC DEFENSE OF MUAY THAI (BID BONG) **96**

Jab '*Bid Bong*' 97

Cross '*Bid Bong*' 99

Body Cross '*Bid Bong*' 101

Overhand Punch (Short and Long) '*Bid Bong*' 102

Kick '*Bid Bong*' 104

Spinning Back Kick '*Bid Bong*' 108

Straight Teep '*Bid Bong*' 110

Side Teep '*Bid Bong*' 112

Elbow '*Bid Bong*' 113

Knee '*Bid Bong*' 115

Using Footwork to Evade the Opponents' Weapons...116

CHAPTER 10 - BASIC THEORY OF RHYTHM (IN MUAY THAI) 119

Basic Theory of Rhythm for Offense 120

Basic Theory of Rhythm for Defense 121
    Step 1 vs. Step 2 Counter-attacks 121

Offensive Rhythm vs. Defensive Rhythm 122

Training the Eyes for the Rhythm of Fighting..122

CHAPTER 11 – THE ART OF MUAY THAI OFFENSE (MAI ROOK) 124

CHAPTER 12 - THE HISTORY OF MUAY THAI 126

CHAPTER 13 – THE ART OF MUAY THAI DEFENSE 129

Razor Toothed Fish..131

Break into the Birdie's Nest 132

The Javanese Lashes His Spear 133

Enao Stabs With His Daggar 134

Prop up Mount Meru 135

Priest bears large Winter Melon 136

Douse the Luminaries 137

The Mon temporarily bears the Foundation 138

Pierce with a Sharp Edged Tool 139

Crocodile thrashes its' Tail 140

Break the Elephant's Trunk 141

Dragon Twists its' Tail 142

Wii-roon-Hoak Returns 143

Break Arawan's Neck 144

Giant Demon King rolls the Realm of the Humans 145

'Tai Yuan' Casting Net for Fish 146

Slice a Squash into Thin Pieces 147

Old Monk Sweeps the Courtyard with a Broom 148

Break the Swans Wing 149

Hermit grinds Medicine 150

Push Against a Pole, Diagonally 151

Lion Crosses a Creek 152

Tattoo a Garland, on the Chest 153

Arawan Swings its' Tusks 154

CHAPTER 14 – LEARNING TO FIGHT FROM BOTH STANCES 155

Footwork Exercise for Developing Your Stance 156

Straight Punch Forward from Square Stance 156

Sharpening Your Step Forward Cross 159

Sharpening Your Cross (Throwing in Place) 161

CHAPTER 15 - THE DAILY TRAINING ROUTINES OF A NAK MUAY 163

CHAPTER 16 - BEFORE YOU START TRAINING MUAY THAI 169

ADDENDUM 171

Additional Defensive Techniques 172

Additional Offensive Combinations 178

The Killing Spots of the Human Body 180

List of the 19 Footwork Movements of Muay Thai 185

EPILOGUE **186**

ABOUT THE AUTHOR **189**

What to Expect from this Book

Learning Muay Thai is a lot like learning a language. For someone starting out to learn English, they'd start by learning the 26 letters of the English alphabet. Then they'd learn to put together basic words. From there they would learn to string together words into sentences. These are the basics which are critical to learning to wield the English language as a tool of communication. From mastery of those basics, comes the power to express, affect and impress upon others through the spoken word.

In the same way the footwork of Muay Thai is comprised of a set of 19 basic footwork movements which are at the base of the most basic and most advanced techniques used in Muay Thai, as we shall see in this book.

'Muay Thai: The Footwork' is written like a text book on the Art and Science of Authentic Muay Thai. We will start by discussing the basic stance, with the intent on teaching the reader to understand Muay Thai through the most important element of training, the footwork.

In Chapters 1 &,2, we will explore the intricacies of the basic Muay Thai stance. From there, we will explore the 19 footwork movements of Muay Thai. After reading these two chapters, you can skip and read any section of the book, and take the value from that chapter because the book breaks down the techniques Muay Thai through the footwork learned in Chapter 2.

In Chapters 3, 4, 5, 6 and 7, you will learn about the basic of Muay Thai – Punches, Kicks/Teeps, Knees, and Elbows and the various ways that each of these weapons can be used to hit the opponent.

After going through the basics of Muay Thai (Chapters 1 – 7), we'll discuss the more advanced concepts of Muay Thai – Basic Defense, Offensive Strategy, and Counter-attacking, utilizing the 19 footwork movements as a common language to break down these techniques.

Chapter 10 will show you how to think about the basic theory of fighting rhythm, describing how the entire fight can be broken down into a series of step sequences carried out between both fighters in a match. This is an important and key concept for understanding how to think about rhythm and timing for executing your offense and defense.

Nothing is new in this book. In fact, it's a direct translation of the standard Muay Thai curriculum in Thailand – seen through the perspective of the footwork. If you're a beginner, this is a great way to start off your training - by learning the Muay Thai arsenal through the most important aspect of Muay Thai training: The Footwork.

If you're intermediate and advanced you might not learn anything you haven't heard or learned before, but you will walk away with a deeper understanding of the possibilities of defense and attack through the footwork of Muay Thai.

Chapter 1 – Starting Point – Breaking down the Muay Thai Stance

Your Muay Thai Stance is the body posture in which all 8 limbs are positioned at the spots where you feel ready to fight. From the stance, you must feel that you have the ability to

1. Move in any direction along the surface of the floor

2. Defend incoming weapons

3. Throw any of your weapons to the opponent at any moment

One of the first priorities of someone starting to learn Muay Thai is learning what it feels like to feel ready to do each of these things from their Muay Thai stance. The proper stance enables you to efficiently use your guards, footwork, and weapons to respond to your opponent.

The Two Fighting Angles

One of the first things to determine about your opponent is the fighting angle of their stance.

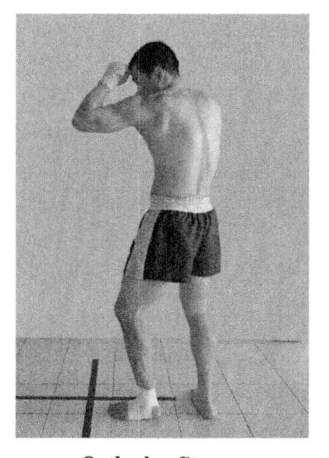

Orthodox Stance    **Southpaw Stance**

1. Orthodox Stance (Left foot is in the Lead, Right foot is in the Rear)

2. Southpaw Stance (Right foot is in the Lead, Left foot is in the Rear)

Is your opponent standing in the 'Orthodox Stance' or the 'Southpaw Stance'? The Opponents' Fighting angle is the stance your opponent feels most comfortable fighting from.

The Feet Position for the Two Fighting Angles

The Feet Position of the Two Fighting Angles creates a stable base at the feet and is the optimal position to feel ready in your Muay Thai stance. The weight of the body is distributed equally over the balls of the feet. For the optimal stance, the position of the feet are slightly turned inward, with the feet making an angle, slightly less than 90°.

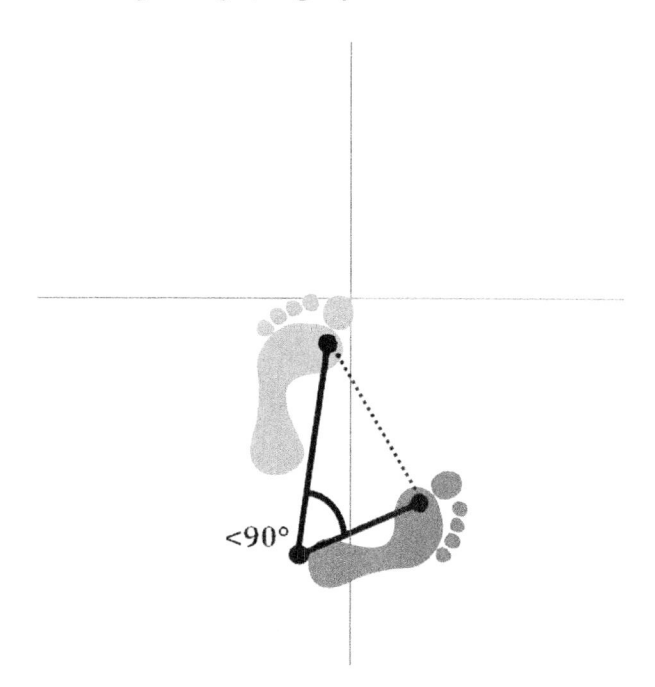

The lead foot is turned in only slightly, so that from your stance, you are still able to lift your lead leg to efficiently check the opponents' kick with your knee or shin. The weight of your body is equally distributed over the balls of your feet.

The Muay Thai Stance – Wide vs. Narrow

The purpose of the Muay Thai stance is to position your body and mind so that you feel ready to perform your defense and offense with the most efficiency. From your fighting angle, broadly speaking, you can position your feet in one of two ways, wide or narrow.

When your stance is **wide**, it means your feet are positioned further apart from the centerline. Standing with the feet in a wide position will naturally make your Muay Thai Stance wide.

When your stance is **narrow**, it means the feet are positioned closer to the centerline (as demonstrated throughout the footwork diagrams contained in this book). Whether you fight from a wide stance or narrowed stance depends entirely on your fighting style.

In theory, a fighter will opt to position their body in the stance that places their preferred weapon of choice in a way that allows them to throw that weapon it to the intended target, fast and heavy.

Pros and Cons of the Wide Stance

Generally speaking, the wide stance, which utilizes wide feet positioning, is optimal for a fighting style which emphasizes superior kicking ability from both legs. This is due to the fact that the wider feet position also positions the hips and shoulders wider, making the chamber of the hip for the lead kick faster and heavier.

The drawback of the Wide Stance is that widening the position of the hips and shoulders exposes more of your mid-line (from your head to your genitals) to the opponent.

Pros and Cons of the Narrow Stance

From the narrow stance, which utilizes narrow feet positioning, kicking from the lead leg is not as efficient because the hips and shoulders are narrower, making the chamber of the hip for the lead kick slower. However, the benefit of narrow stance is that because the feet are drawn closer to the centerline, it exposes less of your mid-line to the opponent.

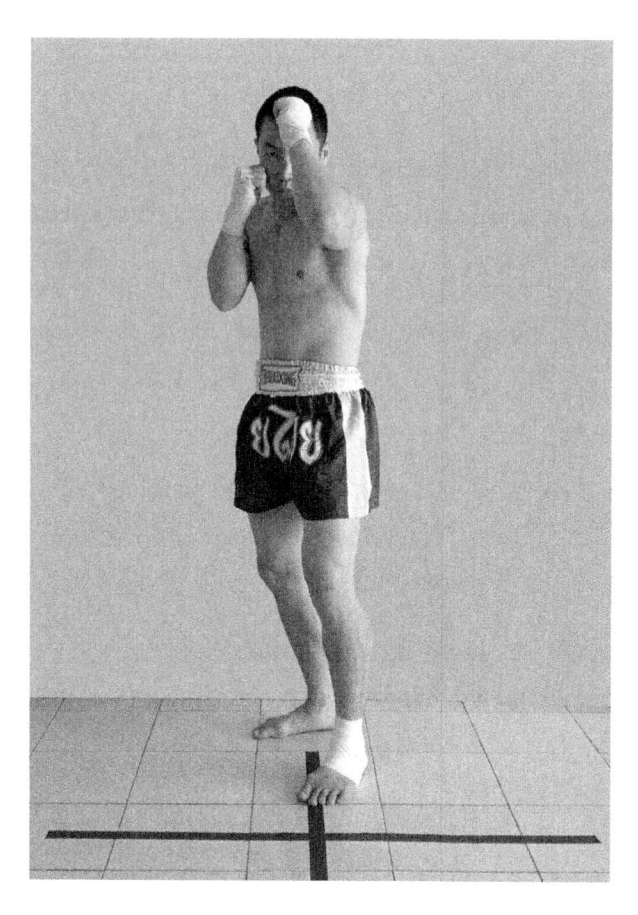

Narrowed Orthodox Stance (Front View)

    A narrowed stance is optimal for a fighting style which emphasizes punching and elbows. From the narrowed stance, the Lead Fist and Elbow are positioned closer to the opponent, making the Lead Hand Punch or Lead Elbow Strike quicker to the target. In particular, the jab, which is thrown directly to the target (typically the face), reaches its' target quicker than from a wider stance.

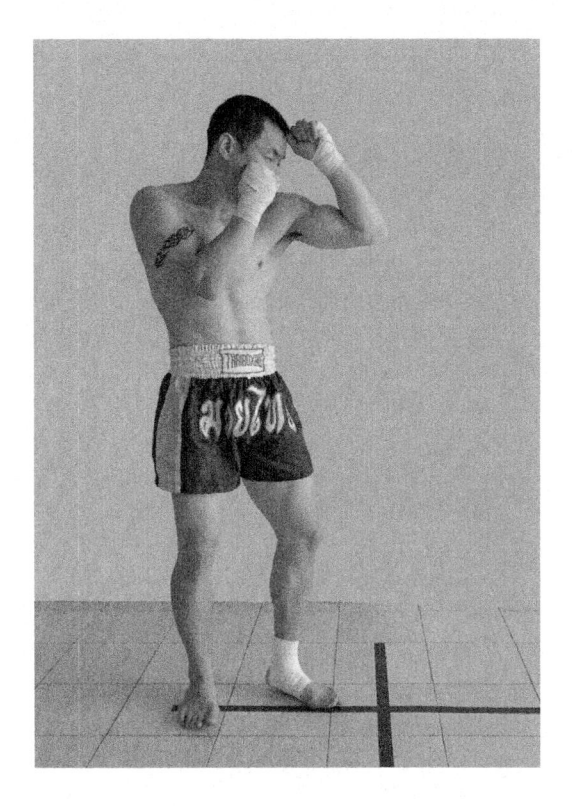

Narrowed Orthodox Stance (Side View)

Additionally, another benefit of the narrowed stance is that the shoulders are positioned with the rear shoulder loaded in the back, which is ideal from throwing a heavy Rear Punch or Rear Elbow Strikes.

Pointing out these differences is not to state definitively which stance, wide or narrow, is better or worse. Each has its own benefits and there are fighters who have learned to fight really well from a wide stance and there are fighters who have learned to fight really well from a narrowed stance.

Generally speaking though, when starting out to learn Muay Thai, it's this authors' opinion that it is easier to start your training learning to fight from a narrow stance. As you develop your skills in establishing a strong Jab and Cross from your Muay Thai stance and fighting from a more defensively oriented narrowed stance, it will be easier to incorporate the benefits of the wide stance into your arsenal as you progress in you skill and training.

The Stance – How to Do it

<u>The Stance Footwork;</u>

In the footwork diagrams below, Left foot is light gray and the Right foot is Charcoal.

1. Stand straight, with your feet apart as shown in the diagram below. Place the foot you feel most dominant with in the rear.

   Right foot in the rear is the 'Orthodox Stance'. **Left** foot in the rear is the 'Southpaw Stance'.

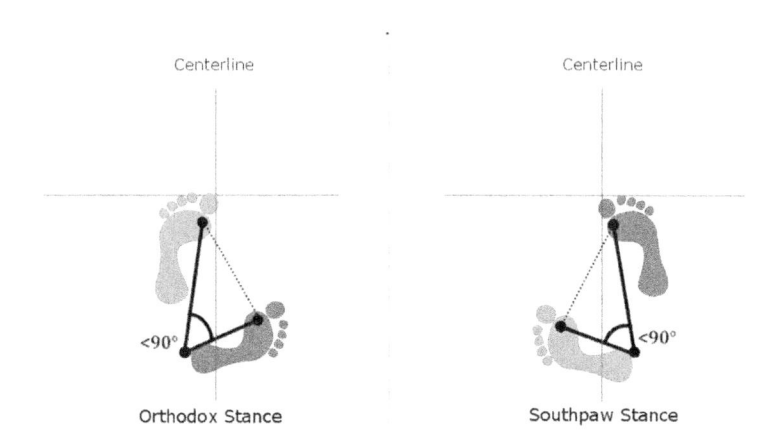

   Centerline   Centerline

   <90°   <90°

   Orthodox Stance   Southpaw Stance

2. For a **wider** stance, stand with the feet further away from the centerline. For a **narrow** stance, stand with the feet closer to the centerline.

3. Position the feet as demonstrated in the footwork diagram above. Turn the balls of your feet inward, so that the feet form an angle, slightly less than 90°.

4. Shift your weight forward over the balls of your feet, distributing your body weight equally onto both feet. When you shift your weight to the balls of your feet, you will feel that your body will shift slightly forward.

   At that point, you'll know that in order to stay balanced, you must bend your knees slightly in order to pull your upper body back to the same position.

<u>Positioning the Upper Body in the Stance:</u>

5. Turn your upper body so that your lead shoulder is towards the opponent and your rear shoulder is away from the opponent. This will give your opponent less of a target to hit.

6. Tuck your chin down, hiding it behind the front of your lead shoulder, with your chin covering the Adam's Apple.

7. Make a light fist with your hands. (Don't clench your fists) Bend your rear arm, tucking the elbow into the body. The rear fist is at the same level as your cheek, slightly in front of your face, with your knuckles the same level as your nose.

8. Lead arm bends up, with your lead knuckles at the same level as your eyebrow. The tip of your lead elbow should be pointing outward toward your opponent.

9. Your eyes look straight by looking over your rear hand, but under the lead hand. The eyes are gazing straight through the opponents' belly. You gaze through the belly because Muay Thai uses weapons from both hands and feet.

If you fix your eyes on the upper body, you won't see attacks coming from the lower body. If you fix your eyes on the lower body, you won't see attacks coming from the upper body. This is why you have to look to the middle.

Chapter 2 - The Art of Muay Thai Footwork

The Importance of Footwork in Muay Thai

Learning the proper footwork in Muay Thai is fundamental to effectively utilizing the weapons of the fist, foot, knee, and elbow. No one is going to stand there and just allow you to hit them with heavy weapons. Before you can land your weapons, you're going to need to learn how to position yourself so 1) you avoid getting hit and 2) so that you are in correct position and distance to throw your weapon accurately to the target.

To land a particular weapon on your opponent, your distance from the opponent must be correct. Without being able to move confidently with your footwork to the correct position of where your weapons will be effective against your opponent, you will never be able to hit your targets with consistency.

So learning the footwork is fundamental to developing skill in Muay Thai. Your Muay Thai instructor teaches you the proper footwork. It is the responsibility of the student to practice the footwork until it becomes subconscious. The beginner student must practice this footwork diligently until he or she knows how to 'walk' in Muay Thai.

It's not enough to just know the footwork movements. The footwork must be practiced until it is subconscious so that when you want to move in a particular direction, it happens without having to think about how to move your feet to get there.

In order to develop this 'sense' of your footwork, drilling and constant sharpening of the footwork is required as part of your Muay Thai training.

Footwork is really important in Muay Thai for doing offense, defense, getting away from your opponents weapons, etc. These all need very good footwork in order to position your body out of the way of incoming weapons or to get into position to land your own weapon.

Presented below are the 19 basic footwork movements of Muay Thai. Similar to learning the English language, with 26 letters in the alphabet, these 19 basic footwork movements are used in combination with the weapons of Muay Thai to make up the offensive and defensive techniques of the art. The remainder of the book will build off of these 19 Muay Thai footwork movements as a tool for teaching the art of Muay Thai.

The 19 Footwork Movement Skills of Muay Thai
(Presented from the Orthodox Stance)

How to Read the Footwork Diagrams in this Chapter

This chapter utilizes footwork diagrams to teach the footwork movements of Muay Thai. Utilize the following key to read all of the footwork diagrams in this book.

The **Black Arrow** indicates the 1st foot movement of the cycle.
The Gray Arrow indicates the 2nd foot movement of the cycle.

The Gray Foot is your Left Foot.
The Charcoal Foot is your Right Foot.

The Numbers on the feet represent the steps in the footwork cycle, with (1) and (2) indicating the starting positions of the feet.

1. Step Forward: (สืบหน้า) Thai Pronunciation: *'Sueb Na'*

Action: Step forward, toward the opponent either to step closer to the opponent or to throw a weapon.

(From the Orthodox Stance) Step toward the opponent, moving both feet forward. Your stance stays the same.

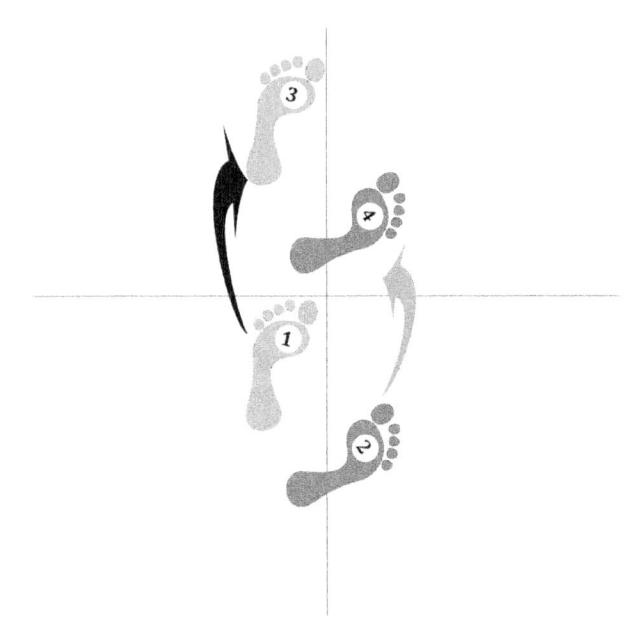

How to Step Forward (From the Orthodox Stance): Left foot (1) is the lead foot and right foot (2) is in the rear. Start by moving your left foot (1) to (3), first. Then move your right foot to follow from (2) to (4). Once you finish one cycle of Step Forward (1-4), your stance stays the same.

Reason to Use 'Step Forward' – Normally, when you are in your stance, you and your opponent are standing outside of the fighting radius and cannot reach one another. Without stepping forward, your weapons won't reach the opponent.

Remarks: The word *'Sueb'* in Muay Thai refers to movement of the feet in which you are moving BOTH feet in the direction you are going.

2. Retreat: (สืบหลัง) Thai Pronunciation: 'Sueb Laang':

Action: Step back, outside of the opponents' striking range.

(From the Orthodox Stance) Move both your feet back one step at a time with the feet moving close to the ground and away from the opponent. Your stance stays the same.

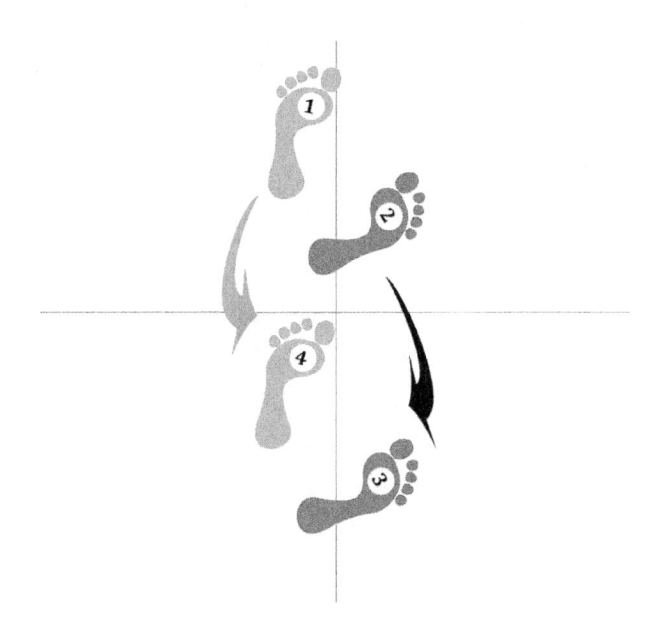

How to 'Retreat' (From the Orthodox Stance): Left foot (1) is the lead foot and right foot (2) is in the rear. Start by moving your right foot (2) to (3), first. Then move your left foot (1) to (4). Once you finish one cycle of Retreat (1-4), your stance stays the same.

Reason to Use 'Retreat: When your opponent attacks you, you can't just stay at the same position, because you don't want to just absorb the force. You can use 'Retreat' to evade the opponents' attack. When you don't know what to do in response to your opponents' attack, you can always use 'Retreat' to evade as long as you are not backed into a wall or corner.

3. Switch Stance Forward (รุกสลับเท้า) Thai Pronunciation: *'Rook Salab-Tao'*

Action: Switch Stances, moving toward the opponent.

(From the Orthodox Stance) Move your rear foot forward, with the foot moving parallel and close to the surface of the ground. Use the ball of the lead foot (1) as the pivot point. After one cycle of Switch Stance Forward, your stance changes to Southpaw.

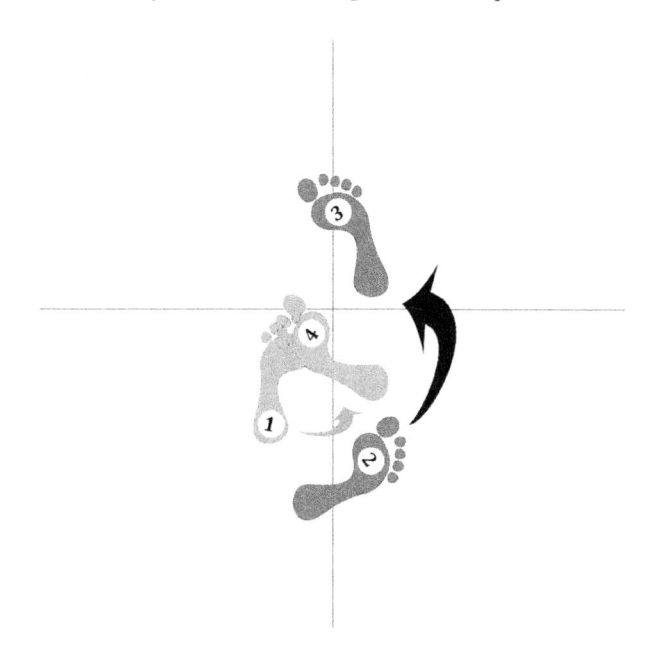

How to do 'Switch Stance Forward' (From the Orthodox Stance) : The left foot (1) is the lead and right foot (2) is the rear. Start by moving your right foot (2) to (3), while twisting your left foot (1) to (4), using your left ball of the foot as the pivot point. After completing one cycle of Switch Stance Forward, your stance changes to the Opposite Stance (Southpaw).

Reason to Use 'Switch Stance Forward' : Use this footwork movement to switch your stance. If you're fighting with an opponent who is good at both stances and you can only move from one stance, you are at a disadvantage. If you have competency from throwing your weapons from both stances, you can use 'Switch Stance Forward' to switch up the game on your opponent.

4. Switch Stance Back (ถอยสลับเท้า) Thai Pronunciation: *'Toi Salab-Tao'*

Action: Switch Stances, moving away from the opponent.

(From the Orthodox Stance) Move your lead foot backward, moving the foot parallel and close to the ground. Use the ball of your rear foot (2) as the pivot point. Your stance changes to the Southpaw Stance.

How to do Switch Stance Back' (From the Orthodox Stance): The left foot (1) is the lead and the right foot (2) is the rear. Start by moving your lead foot (1) to (3), while twisting your right foot (2) to (4), using your right ball of the foot as the pivot point. After one cycle (1-4), your stance changes to the Opposite Stance (Southpaw).

Reason to Use 'Switch Stance Back' – Use this to evade your opponents' weapons. It's faster than using 'Retreat' and allows you to counter attack quicker because you are just pivoting on the back foot and moving only slightly back, just outside of the range of the opponents' weapon.

'***Chawk***' (ฉาก) – The basic Thai translation for '*Chawk*' in Thai means diagonal (45°) or perpendicular (90°). '*Chawk*' as it pertains to Muay Thai, refers to footwork used specifically to evade the incoming force of your attacker by turning your body away from the incoming force to end in a position that is diagonal (45°) or perpendicular (90°) to the original centerline.

In learning Muay Thai, '*Chawk*' is very important defensive footwork.

'*Chawk*' is used specifically in response to your attackers' forward moving force, whether that be stepping forward at you to grab you and clinch up, or throwing a weapon at you. The set of footwork movements comprise of '**1/4 Turn In**', '**1/4 Turn Out**', '**Diagonal Retreat**', and '**Pivot Step**' to evade the incoming force of the weapon.

The reason for learning how to '*Chawk*' is to increase the potential number of ways you can use your Muay Thai weapons to defeat your attacker.

Many of the advanced counter-techniques of Muay Thai utilize '*Chawk*' footwork as you will see in *Chapter 13 – The Art of Muay Thai Defense*.

There are two broad categories of '*Chawk*' in Muay Thai.

    I. 'Chawk Nawk' : Step to **outside** of attackers' arm range.

    II. '*Chawk Nai*': Step to **inside** of attackers' arm range.

I. '*Chawk Nawk*' Meaning: There are 4 ways to '*Chawk Nawk*', based on the direction of your movement of your body to the **outside** of your attackers' arm range by using your footwork.

    1/4 Turn Out (left)

    1/4 Turn Out (right)

    Diagonal Retreat Out (left)

    Diagonal Retreat Out (right)

5. 1/4 Turn Out (left) (ฉากนอกรุกซ้าย) Thai Pronunciation: 'Chawk Nawk Rook (Sai)'

Action: Move your feet forward and to the left, away from the incoming force, outside of the attackers' arm range. In the end position, your body is turned 90° to the centerline.

(From the Orthodox Stance) Start by stepping your Left foot towards the attacker at about a 60° angle with the incoming force (orange arrow), followed by moving the right foot. In the end position, your body is turned 90° to the centerline. Your stance stays the same.

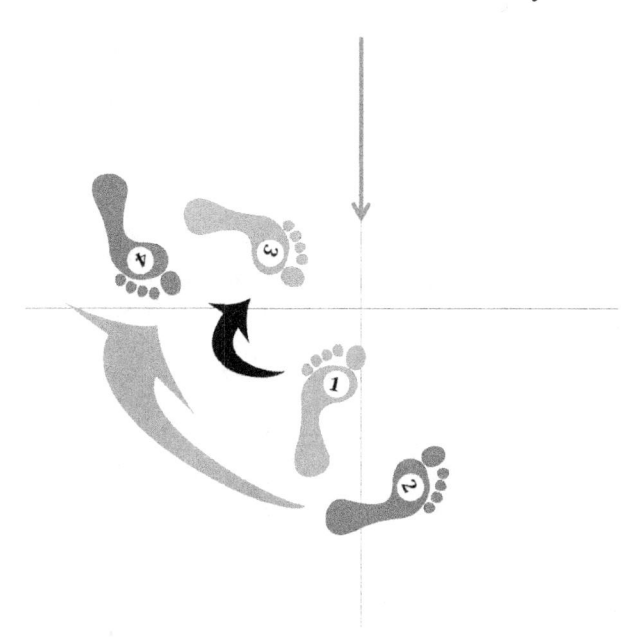

How to do '1/4 Turn Out (left)' (From the Orthodox Stance) Left foot (1) is the lead foot and right foot (2) is in the rear. Move the left foot (1) to (3) and right foot (2) to (4) with your feet parallel to the floor. After one cycle (1-4), you end in the same stance.

6. 1/4 Turn Out (right) (ฉากนอกรุกขวา) Thai Pronunciation: *'Chawk Nawk Rook (Kwa)'*

Action: Move your feet forward and to the right, away from the incoming force, outside of the attackers' arm range. In the end position, your body is turned 90° to the centerline.

(From the Orthodox Stance) Start by stepping your right foot angled to the right, towards the attacker with about a 60° angle with the incoming force of your attacker (orange arrow), followed by your left foot. In the end position, your body is turned 90° to the centerline. Your stance changes to Southpaw.

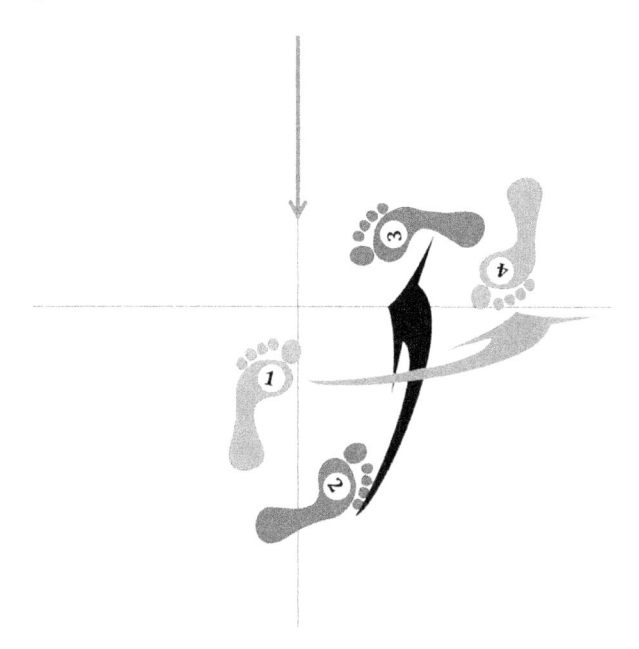

How to do '1/4 Turn Out (right)' (From the Orthodox Stance): Left foot (1) is the lead foot and right foot (2) is in the rear. Move the right foot (2) to (3) and left foot (1) to (4) with your feet parallel to the floor. After one cycle (1-4) you end in the opposite stance (Southpaw).

7. Diagonal Retreat (left) (ฉากนอกรับซ้าย) Thai Pronunciation: 'Chawk Nawk Rup (Sai)'

Action: Move your feet back diagonally and to the left, away from the incoming force, outside of the attackers' arm range. In the end position, your body is turned 45° to the centerline.

(From the Orthodox Stance) Start by pulling the left foot back and away, 45° – 60° from the attackers' incoming force, moving your feet close to the surface of the ground. Pull your right foot to position it in front of the left foot. You end in the Southpaw Stance.

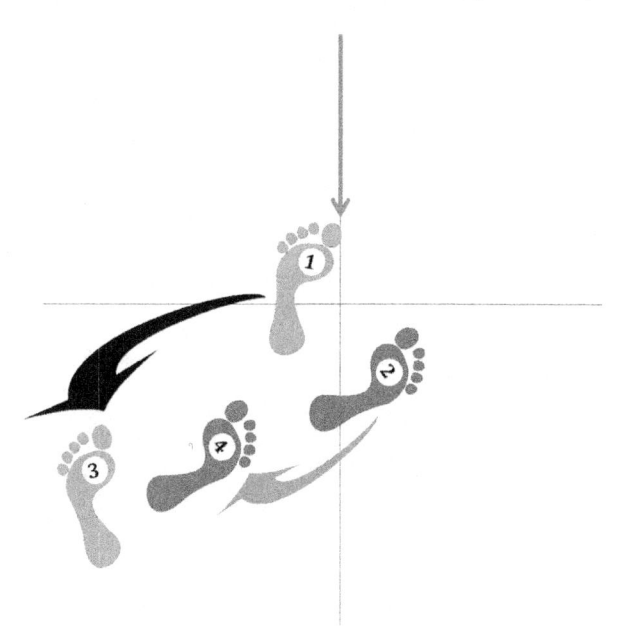

How to do 'Diagonal Retreat (left) (From the Orthodox Stance): Left foot (1) is the lead foot and right foot (2) is in the rear. Pull the left foot (1) to (3) and pull the right foot (2) to (4) moving your feet close to the surface of the ground. After one cycle (1-4), you end in the Opposite Stance (Southpaw).

8. Diagonal Retreat (right) (ฉากนอกรับขวา) Thai Pronunciation: 'Chawk Nawk Rup (Kwa)'

Action: Move your feet back diagonally and to the right, away from the incoming force, outside of the attackers' arm range. In the end position, your body is turned 45° to the centerline.

(From the Orthodox Stance) Start by moving your right foot back and away, 45° – 60° from the attackers' incoming force, moving your feet close to the surface of the ground. Pull your left foot and position it in front of the right foot. Your stance stays the same.

How to do 'Diagonal Retreat Out (right) (From the Orthodox Stance): Left foot (1) is the lead foot and right foot (2) is in the rear. Move the right foot (2) to (3) and pull the left foot (1) to (4) with your feet moving close to the ground. After one cycle (1-4), you end in the same Stance.

II. 'Chawk Nai' Meaning: There are 4 ways to *'Chawk Nai'*, based on the direction of your movement to the **inside** of your attackers' arm range by using your footwork.

One of the major differences between *'Chawk Nawk'* footwork and *'Chawk Nai'* footwork is that for *'Chawk Nawk'* footwork movements you move your body far away from the centerline (and incoming force).

For *'Chawk Nai'* footwork movements, you move near or along the centerline, ending in close proximity to the attacker. *'Chawk Nai'* is separated into 4 types, based on the direction of movement.

Turn In (left)
   a. 1/8 Turn In (left)
   b. 1/4 Turn In (left),

Turn In (right)
   a. 1/8 Turn In (right)
   b. 1/4 Turn in (right)

Pivot Step (left)

Pivot Step (right)

Turn the next page to read about *'Chawk Nai'* beginning with 1/8 Turn In (left)

9a. 1/8 Turn In (left) (ฉากในรุกซ้าย) Thai Pronunciation 'Chawk Nai Rook (Sai)'

Action: Move your feet forward and to the left, away from the incoming force, inside of the attackers' arm range. In the end position, your body is turned 45° to the centerline.

(From the Orthodox Stance) Start by stepping forward with your left foot straight towards the attacker. As your left foot lands, twist your body to make a 45° degree angle with the attackers' incoming force (orange arrow). Your right foot moves and positions behind and close to the left foot. In the end position, your body is turned 45° to the original centerline. Your stance stays the same.

(Note: For this footwork movement, it is even possible to step on the attackers' foot lead foot, a legal move in Muay Thai)

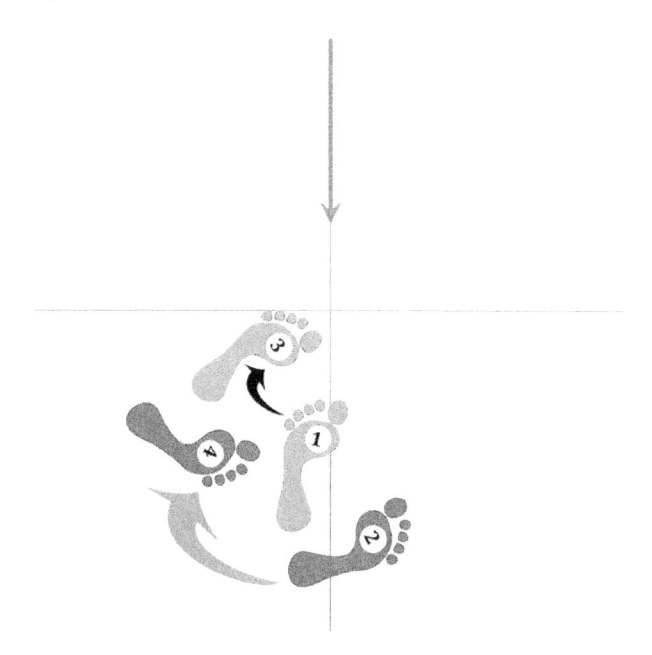

How to do '1/8 Turn In (left)' (From the Orthodox Stance): The left foot (1) is the lead foot right foot (2) is in the rear. 'Move' the left foot (1) to (3) and right foot (2) to (4) with your feet parallel to the floor. After one cycle (1-4), you end in the same stance.

9b. 1/4 Turn In (left) (ฉากในรุกซ้าย) Thai Pronunciation: *'Chawk Nai Rook (Sai)'*

Action: Move your feet forward and to the left, away from the incoming force, inside of the attackers' arm range. In the end position, your body is turned 90° to the centerline.

(From the Orthodox Stance) Start by stepping forward with your left foot straight towards the attacker, with the foot landing turned in at a 45°. (*Note: For this footwork movement, it is even possible to step on the attackers' foot lead foot, a legal move in Muay Thai*) As your left foot lands, twist your body off of the centerline, using the weight of your body to pivot your left foot to make a ≥90° (≥ means equal to or greater than) angle with the centerline. Your stance stays the same.

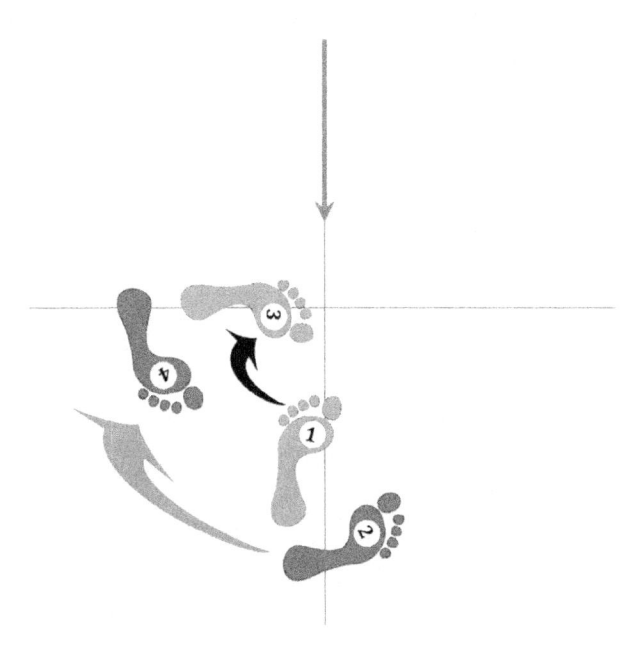

How to do '1/4 Turn In (left)' (From the Orthodox Stance): The left foot (1) is the lead foot right foot (2) is in the rear. 'Move' the left foot (1) to (3) and right foot (2) to (4) with your feet parallel to the floor. After one cycle (1-4), you end in the same stance.

Turn your hips to help twist your body off of the centerline and bring your right foot behind your left foot. In the end position, your body is turned ≥90° to the original centerline.

10a. 1/8 Turn In (right) (ฉากในรุกขวา) Thai Pronunciation: '*Chawk Nai Rook (Kwa)*'

Action: Move your feet forward and to the right, away from the incoming force, inside of the attackers' arm range. In the end position, your body is turned 45° to the centerline.

(From the Orthodox Stance) Start by stepping forward with your right foot straight towards the attacker. As your right foot lands, twist your body to make a 45° degree angle with the attackers' incoming force (orange arrow). Your left foot moves and positions behind and close to the right foot. In the end position, your body is turned 45° to the original centerline (and incoming force). Your stance stays the same.

(Note: For this footwork movement, it is even possible to step on the attackers' foot lead foot with your left foot, a legal move in Muay Thai)

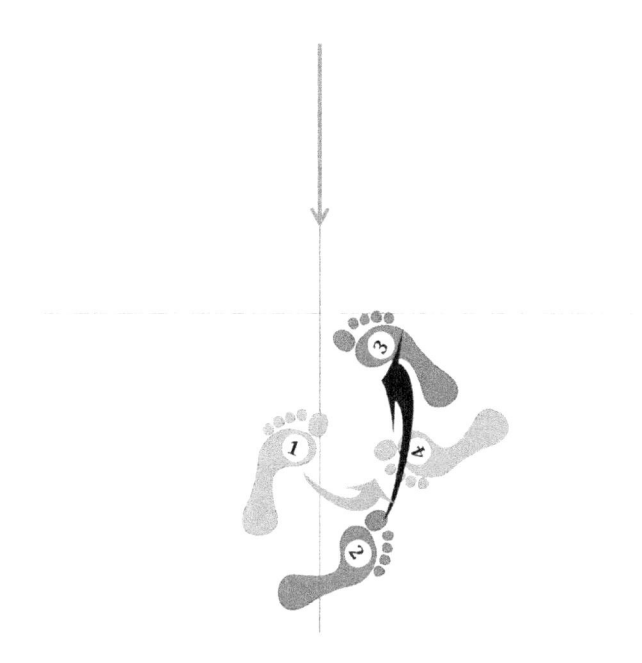

How to do '1/8 Turn In (right)' (From the Orthodox Stance): The left foot (1) is the lead foot and right foot (2) is in the rear. Step the right foot (2) to (3) and left foot (1) to (4) with your feet parallel to the floor. After one cycle (1-4), you end in the Opposite Stance (Southpaw).

10b. 1/4 Turn In (right) (ฉากในรุกขวา) Thai Pronunciation: ***Chawk Nai Rook (Kwa)***

Action: Move your feet forward and to the right, away from the incoming force, inside of the attackers' arm range. In the end position, your body is turned 90° to the centerline.

(From the Orthodox Stance) Start by stepping forward with your right foot straight towards the attacker, with the foot landing turned in at a 45°. As your right foot lands, twist your body off of the centerline, using the weight of your body to pivot your right foot to make a ≥90° degree angle with the attackers' incoming force (orange arrow). Your stance changes to Southpaw.

(*Note: For this footwork movement, it is even possible to step on the attackers' foot lead foot with your right foot, a legal move in Muay Thai*)

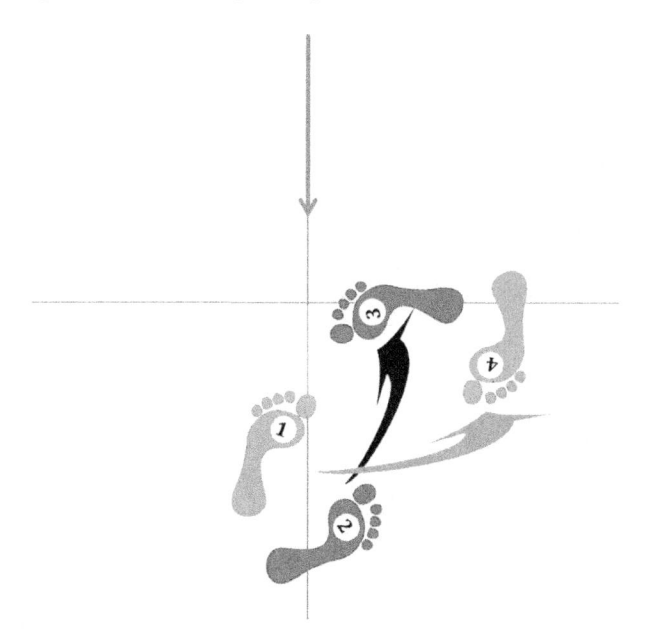

How to do '1/4 Turn In (right)' (From the Orthodox Stance): The left foot (1) is the lead foot and right foot (2) is in the rear. Step the right foot (2) to (3) and left foot (1) to (4) with your feet parallel to the floor. After one cycle (1-4), you end in the Opposite Stance (Southpaw).

Turn your hips to help twist your body off of the centerline as you bring your left foot behind the right foot. In the end position, your body is turned ≥90° to the original centerline (and incoming force).

11. Pivot Step (left) (ฉากในรับซ้าย) Thai Pronunciation: *'Chawk Nai Rup (Sai)'*

Action: Pivot your left foot, away from the incoming force, inside of the attackers' arm range. In the end position, your body is turned 45° to the centerline.

(From the Orthodox Stance) Move your feet to a different position by pivoting your left ball-of-the-foot. Twist your body with the incoming force to make a 45° with the centerline, moving your right foot to the back of the left foot. Your stance stays the same.

How to do 'Pivot Step (left)' (From the Orthodox Stance): The left foot (1) is the lead foot and the right foot (2) is in the rear. Use the left ball-of-the-foot (1) as the pivot point. Twist (1) to (3) and move your right foot (2) to (4). After one cycle (1-4), your stance stays the same.

12. Pivot Step (right) (ฉากในรับขวา) Thai Pronunciation: *Chawk Nai Rup (Kwa)*

Action: Pivot your right foot to bring your left foot behind, away from the incoming force, inside of the attackers' arm range. In the end position, your body is turned 45° to the centerline.

(From the Orthodox Stance) Pivot your rear ball of the foot and move your lead foot to behind your rear foot. Twist your body with the incoming force to make a 45° with the centerline, moving your left foot around to the back of the right foot. Your stance changes to the Southpaw Stance.

How to do 'Pivot Step (right)' (From the Orthodox Stance): The left foot (1) is the lead foot and the right foot (2) is in the rear. Use the right ball-of-the-foot (2) as the pivot point. Twist to (3) and move your left foot (1) to (4). Your stance changes to the Opposite Stance (Southpaw).

Remarks for '***Chawk***' – Whenever you use '*Chawk Nawk*' or '*Chawk Nai*' footwork, your body has end in a balanced position, with the correct stance and correct position of your feet. Remember, '*Chawk*' footwork is used specifically to move you away from the incoming force of the opponent. The position of your feet and your distance from the opponent needs to be just right to evade the opponents' incoming force.

13. Move Feet Around a Circle (การเคลื่อนเท้าเป็นวงกลม) Thai Pronunciation: 'Kluan Tao Wong Glom'

Action: Move your feet in stance around a circle.

Move your feet, one step at a time, moving your feet close to the ground. You can move your feet around the circle, moving either left or right. The center of the circle represents the position of the opponent.

How to 'Move Your Feet Around a Circle (to the Left)' (From the Orthodox Stance): Left foot (1) is the lead foot and right foot (2) is in the rear. Start by moving your left foot (1) to (3), first. Then move your right foot to follow from (2) to (4). Once you finish the cycle (1-4), your stance still stays the same.

How to 'Move Your Feet Around a Circle (to the Right)' (From the Orthodox Stance): Left foot (1) is the lead foot and right foot (2) is in the rear. Start by moving your right foot (2) to (3), first. Then move your left foot to follow from (1) to (4). Once you finish the cycle (1-4), your stance still stays the same.

Reason to Use 'Move Feet Around a Circle' – This footwork movement is used to create an open angle to find a shot.

One major difference between *Move Feet Around a Circle* and '*Chawk*' is that for '*Chawk*' you are turning your body 45° or 90° to the centerline. For Move Feet Around a Circle you are moving your feet along the outside perimeter of an imaginary circle around your opponent.

Slant Step (รุกเฉียง) Thai Pronunciation: '*Rook Shiang*'

Move your body diagonally forward (either to the left or right) toward the opponent to evade the incoming force of your opponent. '*Rook Shiang*' or Slant Step, is an aggressive move toward the opponent at an angle. It is used to step aggressively toward the opponent from one side, evading the incoming force of the opponent from the other side. The foot that moves first, steps forward, 45° - 60° from the incoming force. The following foot will follow in position behind the foot that moves first. There are two kinds of 'Slant Step'.

14. Slant Step (left) - '*Rook Shiang Sai*'

15. Slant Step (right) – '*Rook Shiang Kwa*'

14. Slant Step (left) (รุกเฉียงซ้าย) Thai Pronunciation: '*Rook Shiang Sai*'

Action: (From the Orthodox Stance) Move your left foot 45°- 60° forward to the left of the incoming force (orange arrow). The left foot moves first, with the right foot following behind the left foot, finishing one cycle.

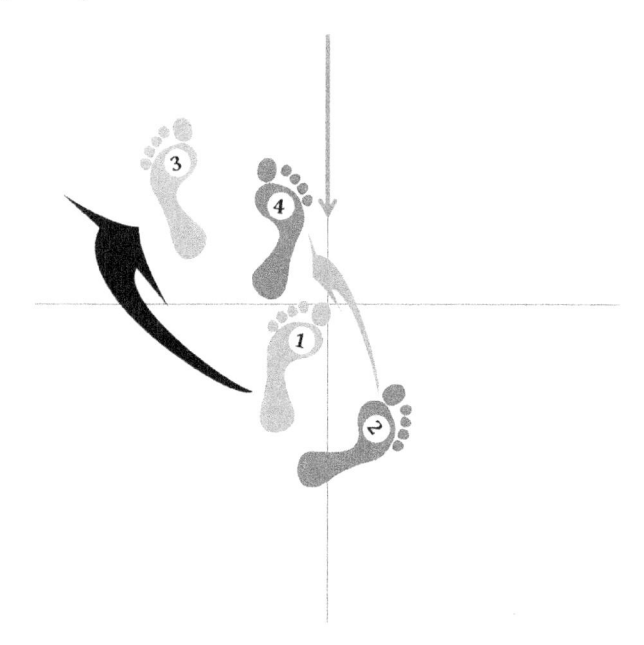

How to do 'Slant step (left)' (From the Orthodox Stance): The left foot (1) is the lead foot and right foot (2) is in the rear. Start by moving your left foot (1) to (3), first. Then move your right foot to follow from (2) to (4). After one cycle (1-4), your Stance stays the same.

Note that when doing *Slant Step (left)* both of your feet end on the left side of the centerline.

15. Slant Step (right) (รุกเฉียงขวา) Thai Pronunciation; **'Rook Shiang Kwa'**

Action: (From the Orthodox Stance) Move your right foot 45° forward to the right with the incoming force (orange arrow). The right foot moves first, with the left foot following behind the right foot, finishing one cycle.

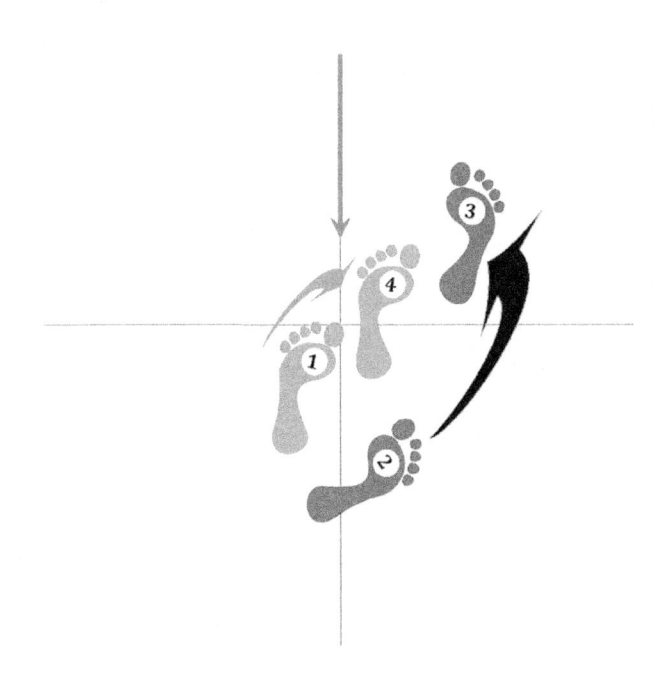

How to do 'Slant step (right)' (From the Orthodox Stance): The left foot (1) is the lead foot right foot (2) is in the rear. Start by moving the right foot (2) to (3) and the left foot (1) to (4). After one cycle, your stance changes to the Opposite stance (Southpaw).

Note that when doing *Slant Step (right)* both of your feet end on the right side of the centerline.

Remarks: When you use 'Slant step (left or right), your body must be balanced and the distance from your opponent where you feet are positioned should be just right. Your body must feel sturdy and compact. This is how you can use 'Slant Step' to defend the incoming force efficiently.

16. Zig-Zag Footwork (ย่างสลับฟันปลา) Thai Pronunciation: *'Yhang Salab Fun Bla'*

'*Yhang Salab Fun Bla*' directly translates from Thai to English to mean 'Step like Razor-Toothed Fish'. The Razor-Toothed Fish analogy is used to name this footwork movement in reference to the zig-zag movement of your body forward along the centerline.

The benefit of the zig-zag movement of *'Yhang Salab Fun Bla'* is that it makes your attack more efficient than just stepping straight forward at your opponent to throw your weapon.

So the concept of *'Yhang Salab Fun Bla'* or Zig Zag Footwork, is approaching your opponent in a zig-zag pattern as to increase the efficiency of your striking while minimizing your exposure to getting hit by continuously moving off of the centerline.

The combinations made up with this sort of zig-zag movement are endless with the variation of punches, elbows, knees, and kicks, available in Muay Thai.

How to do 'Zig-Zag Footwork' (From the Orthodox Stance): The left foot (1) is the lead foot and right foot (2) is in the rear. Start by stepping the right foot (2) to (3) and the left foot (1) to (4) with the feet moving close to the ground.

Next, step the right foot (4) to (5) and the left foot (3) to (6), with the feet moving close to the ground. Your stance changes back to your beginning stance, which is the Orthodox Stance. This finishes one cycle of <u>Zig-zag footwork</u> or *'Yhang Salab Fun Bla'*.

The picture below shows an example of 'Zig-zag' footwork utilizing the Cut Elbow, as an example of how this footwork is combined with the weapons of 'Mae Mai Muay Thai'.

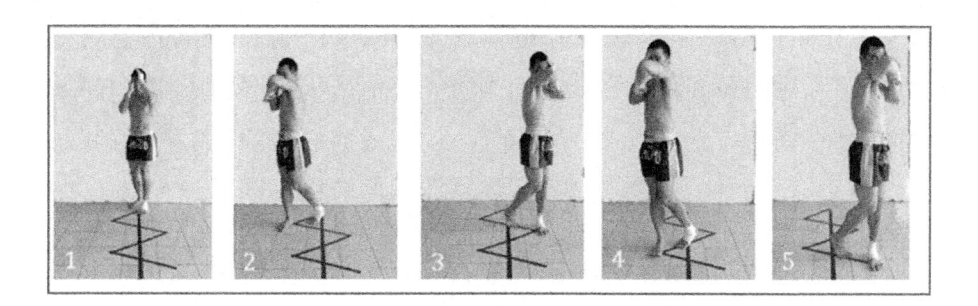

Example of *Zig-zag Footwork* with Cut Elbow

Notice that when performing 'Zig-Zag' footwork, the stance changes from Orthodox to Southpaw, Southpaw to Orthodox, over and over again. You can see this in the picture above.

In step 1, the author starts out in Orthodox Stance, steps to the right into a Southpaw stance to throw the Cut Elbow in Step 2. On Step 3, he steps to the left into Orthodox Stance to throw the next Cut Elbow.

So the 'Zig-zag' pattern of footwork is performed by switching stances at each subsequent step forward into each strike.

17. Parry Mid-line (ย่างสุขเกษม) Thai Pronunciation: *'Yhang SookaSem'*

The footwork of *Parry-Midline* utilizes the *Zig-Zag footwork* we just discussed. The difference is that for *Parry Mid-line*, the footwork is used specifically to evade and parry a straight-attack to the midsection (i.e. – Body Jab, Body Cross, Teep, Straight Knee). For *Parry Mid-line*, you use your hand to parry downward across your midsection, while twisting your hip down and away from the incoming force.

Parry Mid-line to the Left
(Starting from the Orthodox Stance)

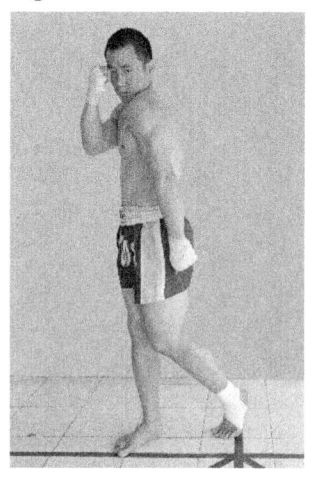

Parry Mid-line to the Right
(Starting from the Orthodox Stance)

18. Lift Knee (ย่างสูง) Thai Pronunciation '*Yhang Soong*' or '*Yok Kao*'

This footwork movement is used to shield the body using the muscles of the leg and knee cap. This footwork is used to block low and middle attacks to body, either thrown angularly at the body (i.e. - Round Kick) or straight to the midsection (i.e.- Teep).

What is commonly known as 'Checking the Body Kick' is an example of a block which utilizes this lift up of the knee to the elbow. The knee can also be used to block the midline from attacks, by lifting the knee straight up to elbow, as shown in the picture below. To perform *Lift Knee*, the knee rises to connect with the elbow.

Lift Knee
(Front View)

Lift Knee
(Side View)

How to 'Lift Knee': Lift your knee, connecting it to the inside of your elbow to cover your belly with your chin tucked down. Keep the hands lifted to cover your face as if you were in your stance.

As you lift your knee up, shift your weight to the other side of body, like a see-saw. Shifting your weight like this, while maintaining a strong base leg will make the calf-muscle and upper leg of your blocking side able to absorb the incoming force.

19. Three Position Stepping (ย่างสามขุม) Thai Pronunciation: *'Yhang Sahm Khum'*

Three Position Stepping, or *'Yhang Sahm Khum'*, is an inherent property of the Muay Thai stance. It's a movement performed by stepping in the direction of the rear foot and changing one's fighting angle, followed by utilizing *Lift Knee* to shield the body from incoming attacks.

Before the standardization of rules for Muay Thai as a competitive sport, matches would take place on bare ground with bumps and uneven surfaces. Fighters would perform the Wai Kru, a pre-fight ritualistic dance performed on the fighting surface. The fighters would use the 'Wai Kru' to survey the fighting surface with their feet for uneven surfaces and ready themselves mentally to fight.

During the Wai Kru, the pre-fight ritualistic dance performed by the fighters inside the ring, fighters demonstrate their *'Yhang Sahm Khum'* with rhythm, fluidity and absolute balance, stepping in a way that you change your fighting angle, while utilizing your *Lift Knee* footwork to shield the body. Experienced trainers can tell just by the quality of a fighters *'Yhang Sahm Khum'* and Wai Kru , their style of fighting and how deeply the practitioner is able to express the Art of Muay Thai.

And so *'Yhang Sahm Khum'* is meant to be practiced with the spirit of dance and aesthetic appeal.

'Three Position Stepping' for Defense: The principle of *'Yhang Sahm Khum'*, or <u>Three Position Stepping</u> for application in combat refers to stepping forward toward your opponent at an angle off the centerline in a way that is narrow and minimizes exposing your mid-line to the opponent.

The footwork concept of <u>Three Position Stepping</u> is utilized in defensive footwork movements <u>Slant Step (Left)</u>, <u>Slant Step (Right)</u>, <u>Parry Mid-line (Left)</u>, and <u>Parry Mid-line (Right)</u> to step off the centerline and away from the opponents incoming weapon.

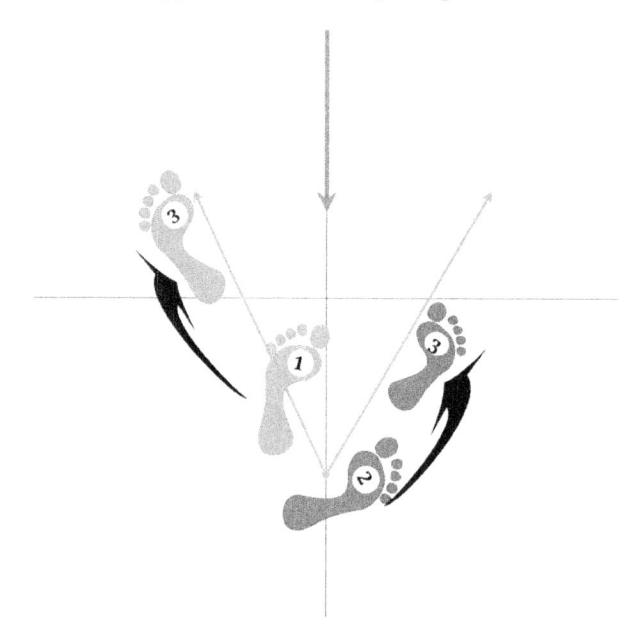

We will see how these footwork movements, which are applications of the concept of <u>Three Position Stepping</u> can be combined with our Basic Defense (Chapter 9 – The Basic Defense of Muay Thai *'Bid Bong'*), the Punches (Chapter 4 – The Art of Using Fists), Teeps and Kicks (Chapter 5 – The Art of Using Foot), Knees (Chapter 6 – The Art of Using Knees), and Elbows (Chapter 7 – The Art of Using Elbows).

'Three Position Stepping' for Cutting Off the Ring

In situations where the opponent is tries to escape out at an angle, *'Yhang Sahm Khum'* can be used to cut off the angles no matter which direction the opponent tries to escape.

Three Position Stepping can be used to cut off your opponents' escape if he attempts to circle away from you, off of the centerline.

How to Cut Off Your Opponent if they Circle Out to the Left

(From the Orthodox Stance):If the opponent tries to escape your reach by moving to your left, use Step Forward, moving to your left to cut off the opponents' escape, as demonstrated in the diagram above. Your stance stays the same.

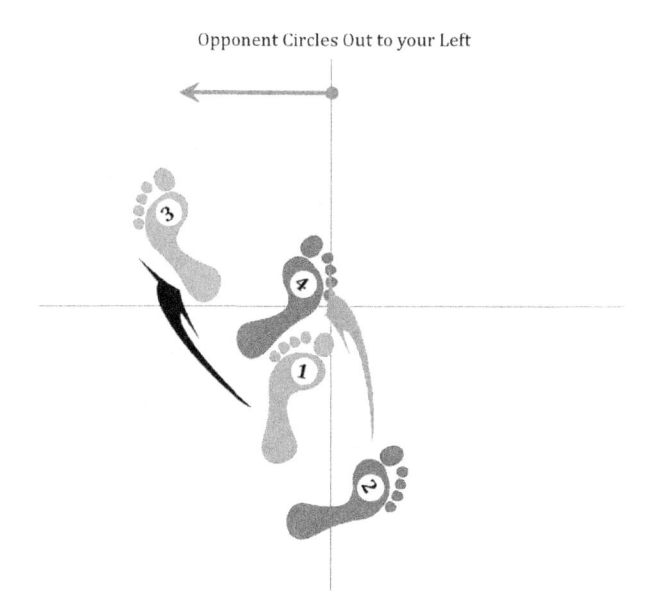

Opponent Circles Out to your Left

After stepping forward, you can use *Lift Knee* with your Left Knee to shield incoming attacks and/or confuse the opponent as to your intentions.

How to Cut Off Your Opponent if they Circle Out to the Right

(From the Orthodox Stance): If the opponent tries to escape your reach by moving to your right, Step with your right foot, in the direction of the opponents' escape.

After stepping forward, you can use *Lift Knee* with your Right Knee to shield incoming attacks and/or confuse the opponent as to your intentions.

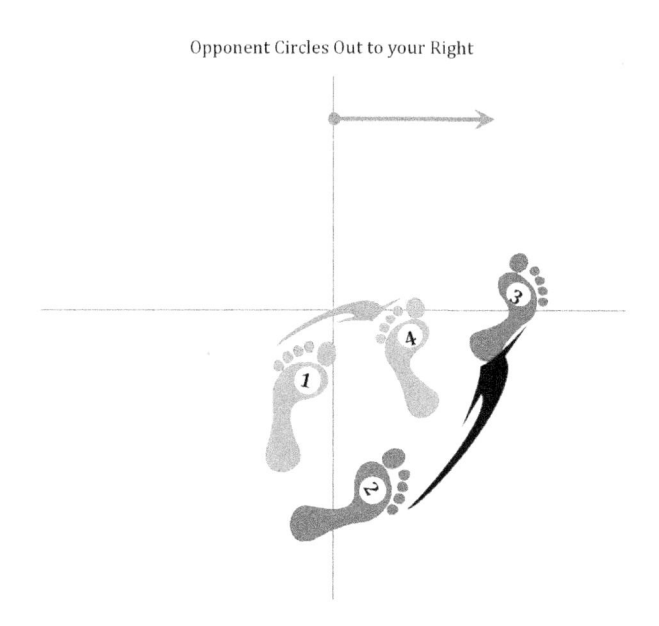

Opponent Circles Out to your Right

If the opponent tries to escape your reach by moving to your right, step with your right foot, in the direction of the opponents' escape. After stepping forward, you can use *Lift Knee* footwork, lifting your Right Knee to shield incoming attacks and/or confuse the opponent as to your intentions.

In Muay Thai, success depends on a fighters' ability to control the action which happens on the centerline, whether that be moving in a way that allows you to land your weapons, or stepping away from the centerline to reduce or evade incoming force. *Three Position Stepping* is a fundamental Muay Thai footwork concept for both Offense and Defense in Muay Thai.

List of the 19 Footwork Movements of Muay Thai

1. **Step Forward**

2. **Retreat**

3. **Switch Stance Forward**

4. **Switch Stance Back**

5. **1/4 Turn Out** (left)

6. **1/4 Turn Out** (right)

7. **Diagonal Retreat** (left)

8. **Diagonal Retreat** (right)

9a. **1/8 Turn In** (left)

9b. **1/4 Turn In** (left)

10a. **1/8 Turn In** (right)

10b. **1/4 Turn In** (right)

11. **Pivot Step** (left)

12. **Pivot Step** (right)

13. **Move Feet Around a Circle**

14. **Slant Step** (left)

15. **Slant Step** (right)

16. **Zig-Zag Footwork**

17. **Parry Mid-line**

18. **Lift Knee**

19. **Three Position Stepping**

Presented above are the 19 footwork movements of Muay Thai. Footwork is important for executing your throwing your weapons, performing your defense, and performing your offense.

The remainder of this book will be presented breaking down the most basic weapons of Muay Thai to the most advanced counter-attack techniques in the Muay Thai Art using these 19 footwork movements as their base.

In Chapters 3, 4, 5, 6, and 7, we will be discussing *Mae Mai Muay Thai* and the basic punches, kicks, teeps, knees, and elbow strikes of Muay Thai.

In Chapter 8, we will be going over the 'Losing Cycle of Weapons' and basic theory as to how each of these weapons relates to one another.

In Chapter 9, we will be discussing basic defense - blocks, catches, parries, and evasions used to defend against the weapons of Muay Thai.

In Chapter 10 – 13, we will be going over the concept of rhythm and how it applies to offensive combinations and break-down some of the more advanced counter-techniques using the 19 Muay Thai footwork movements learned in this chapter.

Chapter 3 – What is Mae Mai Muay Thai?

The beginning phase of learning Muay Thai consists of mastery over '*Mae Mai Muay Thai*'. '*Mae Mai Muay Thai*' literally translates to 'The Primary/Basic Techniques of Muay Thai'. The basic techniques of Muay Thai consists of the basic footwork movements (which we went over in the previous chapter) and the punches, kicks, knee strikes, and elbow strikes.

If you were to make a comparison to learning a language, '*Mae Mai Muay Thai*' would be the 'words' that would make up the vocabulary of that language. It's how you put these basic 'words' together which makes the language effective.

| **'MAE MAI MUAY THAI'** |
| The Basic Techniques of Muay Thai |
| • *The Art of Feet Movement Skills*
 • *The Art of Using Fists*
 • *The Art of Using Feet*
 • *The Art of Using Knees*
 • *The Art of Using Elbows*
 • *The Wai Kru* |

After learning '*Mae Mai Muay Thai*', students are ready to put those basics together to train their Offense and Defense.

The Muay Thai Arsenal - At a Glance

Presented in the chart below is a summary of the types of Punches, Kicks, Knees, and Elbows of Muay Thai. For example, punches are categorized as either Straight or Curved punches. The various types of Curved punches are categorized as either hooks, uppercuts, and overhead punches.

Muay Thai Arsenal (At-a-Glance)

PUNCH	KICK	KNEE	ELBOW
STRAIGHT	**TEEP**	1. Straight Knee	2. Downward Hit Elbow
1. Jab	1. Straight Teep	2. Flare Knee	3. Cut Elbow
2. Cross	2. Side Teep	3. Curved Knee	4. Up Elbow
CURVED	3. Backward Teep	4. Flying Knee	5. Spear Elbow
1. Hook	**KICK**	5. Blocking Knee	6. Tomahawk Elbow
2. Uppercut	1. Straight Kick		7. Reverse Elbow
3. Overhand	2. Diagonal Kick		
	3. Cut Kick		
	4. Arcing Down Kick		
	5. Spinning Back Kick		

The Weapons of the foot include the Teep and the Kick. Knees can be thrown as straight knees, flare knees, curved knees, flying knees or blocking knees. There are 6 types of elbow strikes.

In the following chapters, we will discuss in detail each of the basic techniques of Muay Thai, *Mae Mai Muay Thai*, and the footwork which drives the power in each of them.

In Chapter 3, we will begin our study of *Mae Mai Muay Thai* by going over the 19 basic footwork movements of Muay Thai and how to do them. The footwork of Muay Thai is the most fundamental and important aspect of Muay Thai training. In Chapter 4, 5, 6 and 7, we will discuss the art of using your punches, kicks, knees, and elbows of Muay Thai and how to throw them with proper form and footwork.

Chapter 4 – The Art of Using Fists

How to Make a Fist

Learning how to punch correctly begins first with learning how to form your hand into a fist. By making a fist the correct way, you will protect the bones of your hand from being broken when you punch the target. Most beginners of Muay Thai actually don't know how to make a proper fist and understand why it's important for punching. If your punches are going to damage the target without hurting your own hand, you must learn how to make a fist correctly.

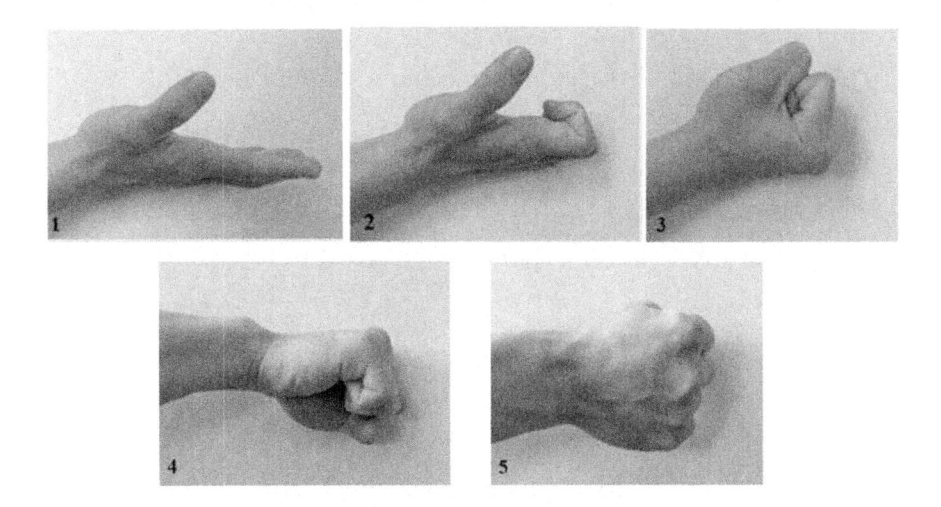

1. Fold the middle joints of the 4 fingers, pressing the fingertips into the base of your fingers
2. Make sure the index and the middle finger are rolled tight.
3. Put the thumb onto the index and the middle finger. .
4. Make sure the ring finger and the pinky are tucked into the palm of the hand.
5. Punch through the target with the knuckles

3 Ways to Position Your Fists for Punching

Fist #1 Straight Fist (หมัดตั้ง) Thai Pronunciation: *'Mahd Thaang'*

This fist is used to throw the punch from the beginning point to the target. This fist, used for the straight punch is fast, without a twist of the wrist. This orientation of the arm is also used to throw the hooks.

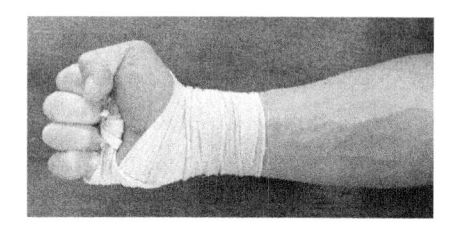

Fist #2 Turn-over Fist (หมัดคว่ำ) Thai Pronunciation: *'Mahd Kwam'*

This fist is similar to Fist #1 but the difference is you turn the wrist down as your fist lands on the target. This way of positioning the fist will result in a heavier punch, but slower than Fist #1 because you twist your wrist down in order to land. This punch is used for the Jab, the Cross, Body Jab, and Body Cross.

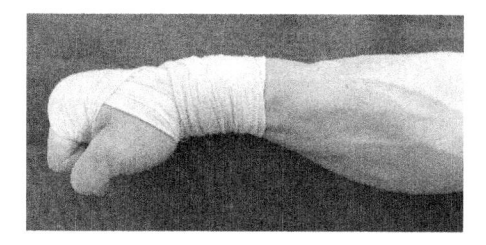

Fist #3 Roll-over Fist (หมัดหงาย) Thai Pronunciation: *'Mahd Ngai'*

The fist is palm-side up. It's a sharp fist, used for uppercuts to reach the target with just the tip of the knuckles.

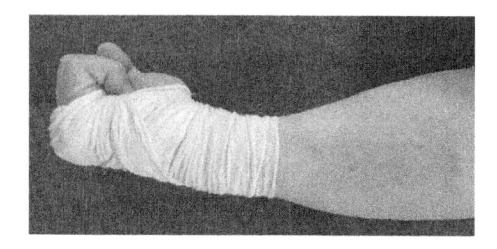

Types of Punches

Punches in Muay Thai are broadly categorized straight punches or curved punches. The straight punches include the Jab (lead hand straight punch) and the Cross (rear hand straight punch). The curved punches include hooks, uppercuts, and overhands. The target of your punches are thrown to either the head or the body.

Straight Punches

1. Jab
2. Jumping Jab
3. Cross

Curved Punches

4. Hook
5. Uppercut
6. Short Overhand
7. Long Overhand
8. Short Uppercut
9. High Uppercut

It's important when intending to utilize the weapons of Muay Thai to know the target for each weapon. Each of the weapons of Muay Thai has an intended target. For example, the fists are used to hit targets on the head and body, whereas the kicks can be used to hit targets on the head, body, and legs. Since knowing the target is a critical piece of information for learning to correctly use your weapon, the targets of each weapon of Muay Thai have been **bolded light gray** throughout the book.

Straight Punches

The Straight punch is a punch that moves from its starting point in a direct line to the target, with accuracy and quickness. It is thrown with either your lead hand (Jab) or your rear hand (Cross). It is a '*Mae Mai*' weapon that is very powerful that can be used in almost all situations. For example, you might be somewhere that is crowded with people – say a restaurant, in the bathroom, or with someone sitting or standing next to you. You can always use your straight punch to defend yourself in those situations if you practice in a correct way.

How to throw the Straight Punch: From your stance, throw your punch straight forward. To step forward into your straight punch, whether it is a Jab or a Cross, you must *Step Forward* with both feet in order to make your punch heavier.

Recommendations for Throwing the Straight Punch:

1. The key to making the Straight Punch heavy when stepping forward is about the timing of your footwork. The foot on the same side of the throwing arm touches the floor the same time the touches the target.

2. Your fist and wrist must be tense and strong and must be positioned straight at the point of contact with target.

3. After you land the Straight Punch, pull your fist back right away. The hand is thrown you're from your eye brow and returns back to the eye brow, following the same trajectory.

4. Your eyes follow the end of your fist to the target and your chin tucks to your shoulder. Land the Straight Punch with your shoulders lined up with the target.

5. The hand of the arm that is not thrown for the Straight Punch is positioned at your face, near your nose.

6. The elbow of the arm that is not thrown for the Straight Punch is tucked to the body throughout the Straight Punch.

Jab

The Jab (or Lead Straight Punch) is a punch that has long length when utilizing your footwork. When using your footwork with *Step Forward* or *1/4 Turn Out (left)* the length of the Jab has the same range as your kick. Compared to the kick, the jab is much faster because it follows a straight trajectory to the target compared to the rotation of the kick to reach its target. Although it is not as heavy of a weapon as the kick, the Jab can be made heavy using your footwork to send your momentum forward into the punch. The target of the Jab is **the face, chin or belly**.

3 Ways to Throw the Jab

(From the Orthodox Stance) The Jab is thrown quick, snappy and concise. It is suitable as an opening weapon to set up multiple hit combinations. The Jab is effective for bothering your opponent in order for you to set-up your next attack. The various forms of the Jab are described below.

1. **Jab without Stepping** – You stay in the same position and throw the Jab. Normally, this jab is weak, but it's very concise and quick, so it is good for opening and bothering the opponent. If you want to make this jab a heavier punch, you need to generate the force by pivoting the balls of the lead foot inward, as demonstrated in the picture above.

    Send the force generated from the lead ball-of-the-foot through your knees, hips, shoulders and shoot it out to the target.

2. **Jab with Stepping** – You throw the Jab as a long range weapon, stepping in to land the jab when your opponent is further away from you. In order to throw this punch,

you need to use *Step Forward*, *Move Feet Around a Circle (stepping left)* or *1/4 Turn Out (left)* in order to reach the target. To make this Jab a heavier punch, as you step into the punch, the lead ball of the foot touches the floor the same time your knuckles touch the target.

3. **Jumping Jab** – This one is similar to 1.2 but the difference is that the rear foot you launch off of is more jumpy. The moment you spring off the rear foot is the same time you release the Jab.

Jumping Jab

How to Use the Jumping Jab (From the Orthodox Stance): The jumping jab is a long range weapon, thrown by jumping forward into the punch, using either *Step Forward* to send it straight or *1/8 or 1/4 Turn Out (left)*, to throw it at an angle. Normally, fighting happens at a shorter range than the range of the jumping jab, making it a very long range weapon.

The key is to start with your feet close, bending at the knees to load up your weight onto the back foot. When landing the punch, your foot hits the floor the same time your fist hits the target. The key to making the punch heavy is learning how to jump forward and send all of your weight through your jabbing arm. If you weigh 165 lbs., you should be able to generate 165 lbs. of weight behind this punch. If your opponent is moving forward the same time you land the Jumping Jab in this fashion, both of your momentums will be added to the weight of the punch and he will feel like he is getting slammed heavily in the face by your Jab.

How to Use the Jumping Jab using *1/4 Turn Out (left)*

Against someone that wants to get close to you to fight such as the '*Muay Khao*' fighter (The Knee Fighter) what they'll want to do to you is get close to you, clinch you up and throw knees from short range. This is an important punch for keeping them away. The Jumping Jab using *1/4 Turn Out (left)* is a surprisingly fast, long range weapon (longer than the kick). Against an aggressive attacker that is moving into your arms range to clinch up, the Jumping Jab using *1/4 Turn Out (left)* can be used to hit the forward moving attacker while simultaneously stepping off the centerline, away from arms of the aggressor.

In order to clinch you up, the '*Muay Khao*' fighter needs to get both hands on you. This requires him to square up his shoulders to get both hands on you. By keeping a narrowed stance and using your Jumping Jab with *1/4 Turn Out (left)*, he will not be able to grab you with both hands.

The Jumping Jab Forward Punch thrown at an angle is an especially important punch for the shorter fighter to be able get around the jab of a taller opponent. Without this punch, the taller fighter will always reach the shorter fighter with the jab first.

Recommendations for when to Throw the Jumping Jab: The distance of this punch is far. The most opportune time to use this jab is as soon as your opponent starts to move in, you take the shot from them, either jumping straight-in with the jab or at an angle. If it lands, their forward momentum combined with your forward momentum will make the Jab very heavy.

How to do the Jumping Jab with *1/4 Turn Out (left)* (from the Orthodox Stance)

1. Start by pulling your feet close and bending at your knees. Shift your weight to the rear foot.

2. Jump off of your rear foot to the left, using *1/4 Turn Out (left)*, throwing the Jumping Jab to the Inner Angle of the opponent.

3. Throw the lead fist out as you jump from the rear foot, using either Fist #1 – Straight Fist or Fist #2 – Turn over Wrist.

4. Send the power of the Jumping Jab to the target by landing your weight heavy onto the lead ball of the foot the same time your fist hits the target.

5. While you are in the air, your rear foot is off the floor, the trunk of your body narrows up, with the shoulders forming a straight line with the target.

6. Your eyes are focused on the tips of the fist, Your chin is tucked to your lead shoulder

7. Your rear hand is positioned, covering your face.

8. The rear elbow is tucked to your body throughout the punch.

9. Once you reach the target, pull your fist back the way it went out.

Cross

The Cross is a rear hand straight punch. From your Orthodox Stance, you throw the jab with your **left hand** and the cross with your **right hand**, which is the rear hand. From your Southpaw Stance, you throw the jab with your **right hand** and the cross with your **left hand**, which is the rear hand.

The target of the Cross is the below the forehead on the face (**eyes, nose, chin**), **jaw-line, temple** and **belly**.

2 Ways to Throw the Cross

The cross can be thrown with or without stepping forward.

Cross (without stepping) – This cross without stepping forward is thrown from a shorter distance. In order to generate power in your cross without stepping forward, you must use the rear ball of the foot (same side as the throwing arm), as the pivot point. The ball of the foot pivots in order to generate force from the foot, sending it to the knee, to the hip, to the shoulder, and through the weapon to the target.

Cross (stepping forward) – This cross is thrown from a longer distance and requires stepping forward and slightly to the left of the centerline using either *Step Forward* or *Slant Step (Left)* in order to 1) send your weight forward into the punch and 2) reach the target with your cross from a shorter distance.

Remarks: When you throw your punches your fists and your feet need to move in good correlation. When stepping forward with your Cross, the foot on the same side as the throwing arm touches the floor the same time the fist touches the target. This is how to maximize the weight behind the punch. This is an example of the 'Same Time' Principle, which you can read more about here.

Curved Punches

Curved punches include <u>hooks</u>, <u>uppercuts</u>, and <u>overhands</u>. When you throw curved punches, your arm is bent at your elbow, and your elbow tenses up.

Hooks

The direction the hook is thrown is from back to front in a circular motion. The punch is thrown with your arm parallel to the floor, at the same level of your shoulder. The hook is a close range weapon. Your fist should not travel too far away from your face. Hit with the knuckles. The hook can be thrown standing in place or stepping forward.

The target of the hook is the **jaw, right in front of the ear,** or the **temple**.

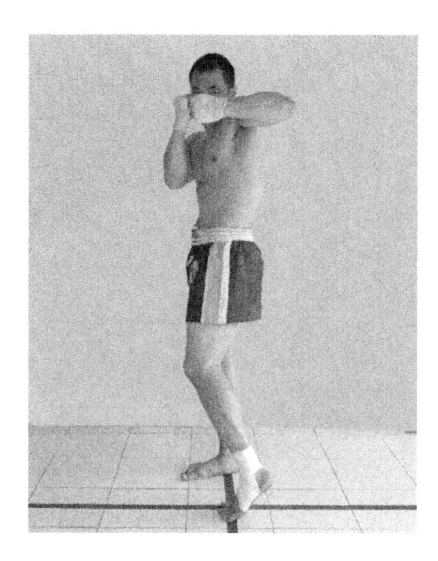

How to throw the Hook (from the Orthodox Stance):

1. Generally, you through the hook when fighting is going on, not as your opening weapon.

2. For short distance, between you and your opponent, you need to send the force from the ball-of-the-foot on the same side of the throwing arm as the pivot point.

3. The arm is bent and your thumb of the fist you are throwing faces your body when you throw the hook.

4. Release your fist, keeping your arm parallel to the floor and your arm at the same level as your shoulder.

5. When you land the hook, your fist should be no further than the length of your upper arm away from your face.

6. The non-throwing fist covers up your chin, with the arm tucked into your body.

7. Once the fist reaches the target, pull it straight back to the original position in your stance.

Uppercut

The Uppercut uses your Roll-Over Fist (Fist #3), throwing the fist from lower to upper as fast as you can. The uppercut is a short range weapon. The force of the uppercut is sent upward from the ball of the foot that is on the same side as the throwing arm. The ball of the foot is the pivot point. If you want to throw this punch from a longer range, you need to *Step Forward* in order to reach the target and increase the weight of the punch.

The target of the uppercut is the **sternum** or the **chin**.

How to do Rear Uppercut (from the Orthodox Stance)

1. Start with your throwing arm bent, making a sharp acute angle and tensing up your elbow.

2. Scoop your rear fist clockwise then upwards to send your knuckles to the target.

3. Your body must twist along with the force that's generated from the foot on the throwing side, by turning the side of your body towards your opponent.

4. The left fist stays at the left eyebrow. The left arm is tucked into the body.

5. When your knuckles hit the target, pull it straight back immediately to the original position.

6. You can throw the right uppercut standing in place, using the ball of the foot as the pivot point or you can *Step Forward* into the punch. It depends on the distance between you and your opponent.

Remarks: To maximize the damage of the rear uppercut (from the Orthodox Stance) scoop the throwing fist towards the opponents belly in a clockwise direction then straight up to the chin of the opponent.

Short Uppercut

The Short Uppercut is an upwards punch in which you start by first lowering your hips by bending your knees to position your body to send the force up with the punch. The Short Uppercut is used in very close distance fighting, moving in towards the opponent from a lower position, with a bend at the knees. Use this bent position of the knees to drive the punch higher with your legs as you throw Short Uppercut straight up to the target.

The target of the Short Uppercut is the **sternum** or the **chin**.

How to do Lead Short Uppercut (from the Orthodox Stance)

1. There are two steps to Short Uppercut. The first step is to lower the position of your body slightly. The second step to deliver the punch by pivoting on the ball of your foot to send the force upward to the target.

2. Step 1 - Starting by bending at the knees, stepping forward to close the distance. You are approaching the opponent from a lower position.

3. Step 2 – To release the punch, push upwards with the legs into the punch.

4. Keep the throwing arm bent throughout this punch.

5. Your elbow is an acute angle and tucked toward your body

6. The punch starts from the beginning point up using the force from the balls of the foot of the throwing arm, using the pivot to send the force up to the knee, hip, shoulder and through to the punch

7. The front part of the fist, turns in towards to face your body (knuckles facing the opponent). The distance of the fist away from your face is about the distance of your upper arm.

8. Rear fist (the non-throwing arm) is positioned next to your eyebrow.

9. For Short Uppercut, you can do standing in place, or stepping toward the opponent, depending on the distance between you and your opponent

Remarks:

1. To inflict maximum damage with Short Uppercut, the fist of the throwing arm is thrown along the straight line between the opponents belly button straight up to the chin, following that trajectory.

2. The difference between Short Uppercut and the Uppercut is that Short Uppercut is thrown from a lower position moving to a higher position to reach the target at a very close distance. The trajectory is almost straight up with the knuckles of your fist landing on the target. The distance from your opponent is no further than the length of your upper arm. The Uppercut is thrown with a scooping, clockwise or counter-clockwise motion, depending on the arm being used to throw the punch. The scooping, clockwise/counter-clockwise trajectory of the uppercut allows it to weave underneath the opponents arm to reach the chin.

High Uppercut

High Uppercut is an upwards punch that's performed by throwing the fist from your chin straight to the target. The benefit of this punch is that it can be thrown against someone that is taller than you.

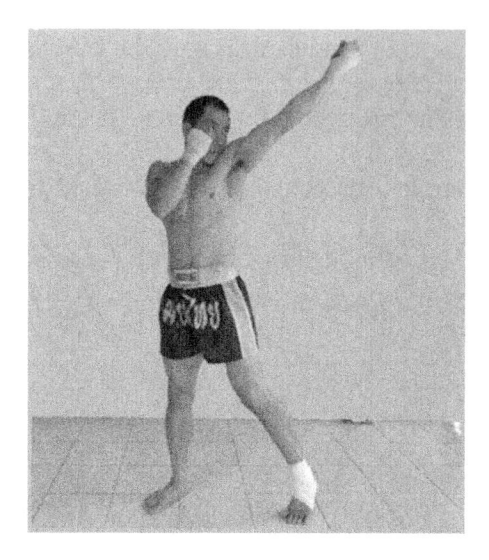

The target of the High Uppercut is the **chin** or the **throat (Adam's apple)**.

How to throw the Rear High Uppercut (from the Orthodox Stance)

1. Start by positioning both arms (upper and lower arms) at acute angles.

2. The lead fist is at the eyebrow. The rear fist at the cheek, with the knuckles at the level of your nose

3. Throw Rear High Uppercut straight forward and up using Fist #3 (Roll-over Fist) without bending the knees. The fist travels from your chin straight to your opponents chin.

4. The fist, the elbow, the arm, of the throwing arm is straightened, tense, and strong at the point of contact.

5. Your body twists according to the twist of your ball of the foot on the throwing side. Turn the side of your body according to the twist of the ball of your foot. The side of your body turns forward into your opponent, before releasing the rear fist from your face to the target.

6. You can throw the High Uppercut standing in place, or using *Step Forward* to reach the target, depending on the distance between you and your opponent

7. After you hit the target, return your body immediately back to stance.

Short Overhand

The short overhand is a punch that is thrown downward at a diagonal angle, with the arm bent at an acute angle (<90°), with the palm side of the hand facing you. Land with the knuckles. The short overhand can be thrown standing in place, using either *Step Forward* or *1/4 Turn In (left)* for the left overhand or *1/4 Turn In (right)* for the right overhand.

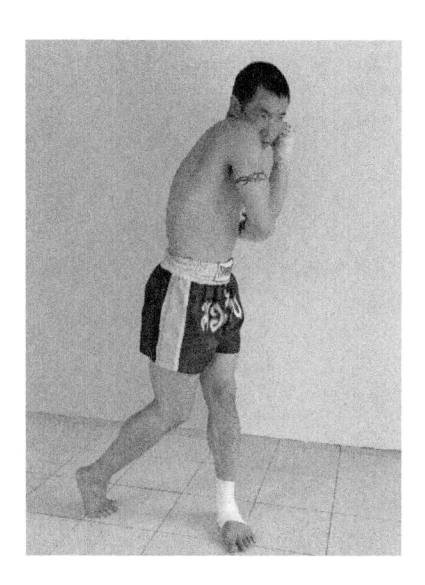

The target of the short overhand is the **jaw, right in front of the ears,** and **temple**.

How to do Right Short Overhand (from the Orthodox Stance):

1. Bend the arm in an acute angle, and tense the elbow.

2. Throw the overhand punch, with the elbow joint at an acute angle (<90°), from top down, by using your body weight to make the punch heavy.

3. Your Right Shoulder tucks to your right ear as you throw the punch.

4. Throw the punch, wrapping the arm around your body, as if to swing completely through the target.

5. Land on the target with your knuckles.

6. For the short overhand, when you use it with '1/4 Turn In', in order to help to increase the force to the punch, you need to turn the hip into the overhand.

7. When you throw the short overhand from the same position without stepping, twist the ball of the foot on the same side of the throwing arm in order to generate more force. Use the twist of the ball of the foot to send the force through your knees, hip, and shoulders and through the punch

8. Once your knuckles hit the target, pull it back to the original position.

<u>Long Overhand</u>
The Long Overhand is similar to the short overhand.

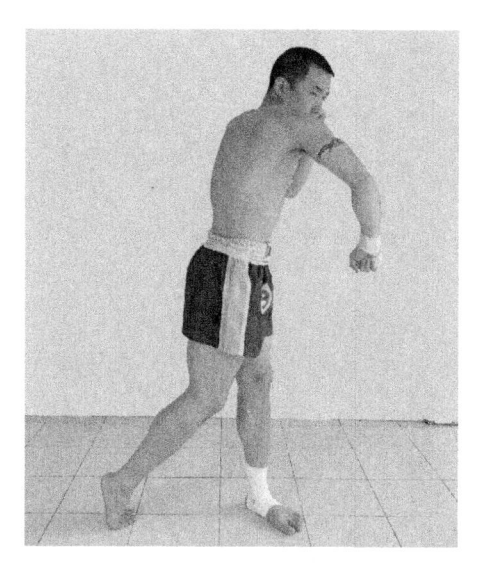

Similar to the Short Overhand, the target of the Long Overhand is the **jaw, right in front of the ears,** and **temple.**

There are a few differences between the short and long overhand.

1. For the long overhand, you stretch your arm out more than the short overhand. The angle of your elbow is obtuse (>90°) or almost straightened out.

2. Just like for the Short Overhand, you can throw the Long Overhand using *1/4 Turn In (left)* for the left overhand or *1/4 Turn In (right)* for the right overhand. The difference is that you need to step off the centerline a bit more .

3. Once your knuckles touch the target, pull your hand back to your original spot.

Remarks: There is a special kind of overhand punch which is similar to the long overhand we just talked about. The difference is you hit the target with your wrist. The target of the wrist is the **neck, ears, and temples**.

Developing Hand and Foot Correlation for Punching

For punching, it's important for power and balance to correlate the movement of your hands with the movement of your feet. Regardless of whether you throw your punch standing in place or stepping forward, the power generation always starts at the ball of the foot on the same side of the throwing arm. This is an important concept. Another way of thinking of it, is that the feet control the movement of the upper limbs.

The Principle of 'Same Time'

If you throw a punch with your **left fist**, then your **left ball of the foot** must be touching the ground heavy, the same time the knuckles hit the target.

If you throw a punch with your **right fist**, then your **right ball of the foot** must be touching the ground heavy the same time the knuckles hit the target.

Punching with this hand and foot rhythm will help send the weight of your body into the punch while helping to maintain proper balance. Remember,

This principle of landing the ball of the foot and the fist the same time applies also to the elbows. If you throw your **left elbow**, your **left ball of the foot** must touch the ground heavy the same time the elbow hits the target.

For exercises on how to develop proper rhythm between your hands and your feet for your punches and elbows, click to Chapter 14 – 'Learning to Fight from Both Stances'

Chapter 5 – The Art of Using Foot

In Muay Thai, the weapons of the foot are the Teep and the Kick. The kick is an angular attack which is thrown by rotating the body to swinging the leg toward the opponent (like a bat) to hit the opponent with the shin, the top of the foot, or the heel. The surface that you strike with depends on the type of kick thrown.

The Teep is a straight attack. It is a foot thrust which involves chambering your leg up and using your hips to send the leg out towards the opponent, hitting the opponent with the toes, heel, the ball of the foot or the full foot.

The Difference Between the Teep and The Kick

Teep	**Kick**
Chamber your leg, then thrust your hip, to send your leg to the opponent	Push off your foot to send your leg forward, twist your hips and body to swing your leg to the opponent
Straight Attack (Foot Thrust)	Curved Attack (Swing Your Leg)
Hit with the toes, heel, the ball of the foot, or full foot	Hit with the shin, top of the foot, or heel

Kicks

The Kick is the heaviest weapon and is used at long distance from the opponent. There are 5 basic types of kicks.

1. Straight Kick
2. Diagonal Kick
3. Cut Kick
4. Arcing Up and Down Kick
5. Reverse Kick (Spinning Back Kick)

Straight Kick

The straight kick is thrown from your stance to the target, in the direction perpendicular to the floor by using the top of the foot or the shin to hit the target.

In ancient times, when Muay Thai was used on the battlefield, the target of the Straight Kick would be either the **groin** or the **chin**. As a sport, the target of the Straight Kick is the **chin**.

How to do the Rear Straight Kick (From the Orthodox Stance)

1. Step Forward and swing the right upper leg up, perpendicular to the floor.

2. Straighten your right leg, using your rear shin or top of your foot to hit the target.
3. Left hand is used to cover your face and chin.
4. Right arm swings to the back in the opposite direction of the kick
5. Lean your body back if the target is high
6. Tense the ab muscle in order to make the straight kick more powerful
7. Send the force from the rear foot by lifting it upward to the target.
8. Once you finish kicking, pull the leg back and position yourself back into stance

Diagonal Kick

Normally, the Diagonal Kick is thrown, landing with the top of the foot, fast and snappy as an opening weapon. Because it's an opening weapon to setup a combination after landing the shot, you need to be able to return to your stance with a strong base in order to continue throwing more weapons. The Diagonal kick can be thrown either by folding your knee first and then slapping the rest of your leg to the target, or you can throw it like a flared kick, with the kick thrown with the leg nearly straightened. The benefit of using the Diagonal Kick is that it's fast and snappy.

The target of the Diagonal Kick is the **lower rib cage**.

How to do the Diagonal Kick:

1. Bend the knee of the kicking leg as you lift it up. Then, slap the ball of your kicking foot out to the target.

2. When you throw the diagonal kick, either with the folded knee or the flared leg, in order to increase the force of the kick, you need to turn your hip into the kick.

3. The angle of the kick must be narrow to the centerline because kicking the leg wide will make you lose balance and will make the kick slow to reach the target.

4. Use the left hand to cover your face and chin.

5. After you finish kicking, pull your leg back and end back in perfect stance, with a strong base.

6. The kick can be thrown standing in place or stepping forward to increase the length and power of the kick.

The Cut Kick

This kick is called 'Cut Kick' because it 'cuts' straight across the target, parallel to the ground. The Cut Kick is stronger than the Diagonal kick, because it utilizes the whole weight of the body. There are two kinds of Cut Kicks.

1. High Cut Kick

    1.a   *'With the Flow of Water'*

    1.b   *'Against the Flow of Water'*

2. Low Cut Kick.

High Cut Kick

The high cut kick utilizes the whole body to kick by swinging your leg curving upward to the target. The kicking leg can be bent or straightened out as you land the kick. Use your shin to hit the target. The cut kick is a very heavy kick if you learn how to put all of your weight behind it.

The target of the High Cut Kick is above the waist - to the head, (**neck, jaw, temple**), the body (**lower rib cage**) or the **upper arms**.

Two Ways of Hitting with the High Cut Kick

1.a. *'With the Flow of* Water': Kicking the opponent in the direction of his forward momentum

The above picture depicts the concept of kicking the opponent *'with the flow of water'*.

The Attacker (red shorts) steps forward to throw the Jab. At the same time, the Defender (blue shorts) uses *Diagonal Retreat (right)*, leading with the right foot, to step away from the Jab. The Defender follows up with a right High Cut Kick to the Attackers' body, sending the force of the kick in the same direction that the Attackers' is moving to throw the Jab. This is an example of kicking the opponent '*with the flow of water*'.

1.b. '*Against the Flow of Water*': Kicking against the forward momentum of the opponent.

The above picture depicts the concept of kicking the opponent '*against the flow of water*'. The Attacker (red shorts) steps forward to throw the Cross. At the same time, the Defender (blue shorts) uses *Slant Step (left)* , stepping forward and to the outside of the cross with the left foot and throwing the High Cut Kick with the right foot. The High Cut Kick hits the Attackers' body, as he moves forward to throw the cross. This is what is referred to as kicking the opponent '*against the flow of water*'.

Low Cut Kick

The Low Cut Kick is similar to the high cut kick but the difference is when you kick, you bend the knee of the supporting leg in order to shift your body weight lower to hit the lower limbs. Lowering the body, while stepping to the side allows you to attack the opponents lower limbs while at the same time avoiding the opponents' high attacks by moving low and to the side. The shin is used to hit the target. The target of the low cut kick is the **quadriceps muscle, the inside knee joint**, and the **outside of the knee joint**.

If throwing the Right Low Cut Kick, use *Slant Step (left)*.

If throwing the Left Low Cut Kick, use *Slant Step (right)*.

Right Low Cut Kick to the Outside of the Knee Joint using *Slant Step (left)* (Orthodox Stance)

Left Low Cut Kick to the Inside of the Knee Joint using *Slant Step (right)* (Orthodox Stance)

Arcing Down Kick

For the 'Arcing Down Kick' you swing your legs in a curved trajectory up to down, twisting your foot in order to reach the target. The foot travels upward clearing the shoulders of the opponent and then arcs down onto the neck with the crook of the ankle or shin.

The target of the 'Arcing Down Kick' is the **neck**.

How to do Rear Arcing Up and Down Kick (from the Orthodox Stance):

1. Swing the right leg upwards in a circular motion

2. Once you reach the highest point of the circular trajectory, twist the right foot down in order to hit the target (neck).

3. Use the left ball of your foot, which is the base foot, as the pivot point in order to help with twisting the crook of the ankle down onto the neck.

4. The right arm swings outward in the opposite direction of the kicking leg.

5. The left hand stays tucked to the left eyebrow. The left elbow and arm are positioned a little bit wide and away from the body.

Technique: To land the 'Arcing Up and Down Kick' onto the opponents neck, misdirect your opponent by looking down at their feet. As soon as they drop their hands, throw the kick down onto the neck.

Spinning Back Kick

The Spinning Back Kick is thrown typically in combination with a missed high or low cut kick.

The target is the **neck, jaw, temple, ribs,** and **arms**.

How to do the Spinning Back Kick:

1. After a missed High cut kick or low cut kick, place the kicking foot that just missed the target down and turn your body backwards, swinging the other foot up and backwards in a curved trajectory. Use your heel to land the target

2. After you finish the turn, you should be facing your opponent.

Teeps

The Teep is thrown by chambering your leg up and then thrusting the hips forward to your lower leg at the target. The Teep is a long range weapon which gets its' length from the extension of the legs, the drive of the hips forward, and slight lean of the upper body. There are 3 kinds of Teep.

1. Straight Teep
2. Side Teep
3. Backward Teep

Straight Teep

For the straight Teep, you must lift your foot up to chamber the hips then send the foot forward to reach the target with your (1) toes, (2) ball of your foot, (3) sole of your foot, or the (4) heel.

The target is the **top of the leg, the body,** or **the face.**

How to do the Lead Straight Teep (from the Orthodox Stance)

1. Start with both hands up in the correct stance position.

2. Chamber the hips. To chamber the hips, lift your leg up. Lift the chambered leg up as high as you can.

3. To create a stronger chamber of the leg, as you lift the leg, flex the ball of the foot of the Teeping leg inward toward the supporting leg. From that chambered position, throw the Teep.

4. The hand on the same side of the Teep leg swings in the opposite direction of the Teep. The other hand stays at the eyebrow, the arm tucked into the body

5. After you Teep, pull the foot back the same way it went out and then return to your original stance.

Things to remember about the Straight Teep:

1. For the straight Teep, you can Teep high or low, it depends on how you chamber. If you chamber high, you can Teep high. If you chamber low, your Teep is going to be low.

2. The power of the Teep depends on the springiness of the supporting leg to send the force forward through the hips.

3. When you throw the lead Teep, to generate more power, twist the supporting foot.

5 Types of Straight Teep

1. **Regular Straight Teep** (*'Teep Throng'*) This is the basic straight Teep.

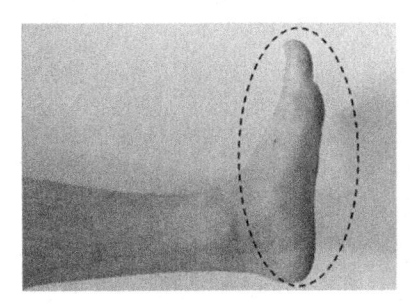

   Hit the target with a flat foot.

2. **Pecking Teep** *('Teep Jig')*

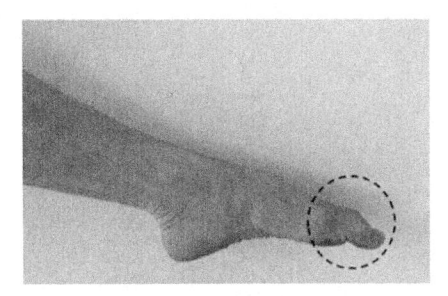

   This is a kind of Straight Teep that is used to defend by tensing the toes down and throwing the Teep towards the target hitting downward onto the target.

   The target is the **quadriceps muscle** or the **belly button**.

3. **Push Teep** (*'Teeb Neb'*) This Teep uses the ball of the foot to Teep to the target.

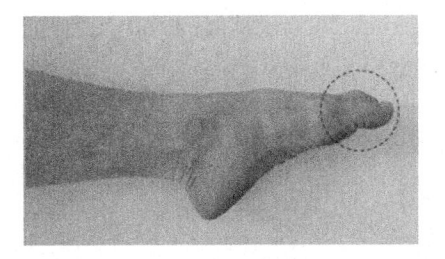

Normally, this is done with the lead foot. This can be used as an opening weapon because it can be thrown quickly while maintaining a strong base.

4. **'Front Kick'** (*'Teep Sot'*) This is actually more similar to the straight kick than a Teep because there is no chamber.

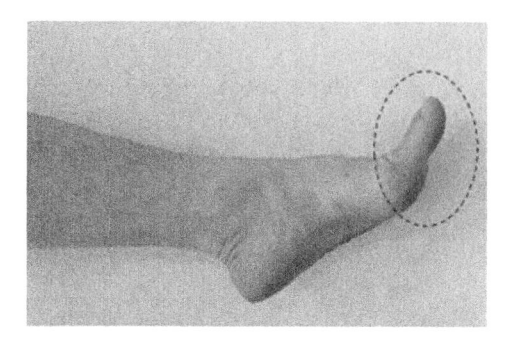

This is a very heavy kick which is landed with the ball of the foot, thrown will a flexed foot, toes curled up. It's a very effective weapon for taller fighters.

The target is the **gallbladder** or the **chin**.

5. **Heel Teep** (*'Teep Ting'*) This is a straight Teep thrown with the rear foot, landing with the heel.

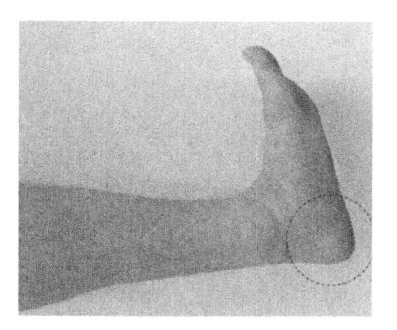

Normally the Heel Teep is used as a follow-up weapon because it uses the powerful rear leg and heel to hit the target. To land with just the heel, you need to throw the Teep by pulling your toes back on the rear foot as you throw it forward. The Heel Teep is thrown with no chamber. To make the Heel Teep powerful, you need to shift your body weight forward over the lead foot.

Side Teep

The Side Teep is thrown by chambering your leg and twisting your body sideways to land with your heel or the side of your foot. The leg is chambered to the side of your body instead of in front of the body like for the straight Teep. The Side Teep generates power similar to that of the knee strike, but it's longer. It is a good defensive weapon.

When used for offense, the target of the Side Teep is the **body**.

When used for defense, the target of the Side Teep is the **knee joint, quadriceps muscle**, or the **side of the ribs**.

How to Side Teep (From the Orthodox Stance):

1. Start from a perfect stance

2. Chamber the leg up to the side of your body, lifting it as high as you can.

3. Turn your body down the same time you throw the Teep, narrowing up the hip, shoulders, and head in a straight line, about parallel to the ground.

4. Twist the ball of the foot of the Teeping leg downward in order to make the Side Teep land with the heel or the side of the foot.

5. Twist the hip down to reach the target so that your leg is still parallel.

6. After you throw the Teep, come back to your stance.

Technique: Jumping forward into the Side Teep makes it reach the target faster than throwing it from your standing position.

Backward Teep

The Backward Teep is a reverse Side Teep. The target of the Backward Teep is the **belly**.

How to Backwards Teep (From the Orthodox Stance):

1. Both hands positioned in the perfect stance position

2. Chamber as high as you can with the lead leg, similar to as if you were throwing the straight Teep or Side Teep

3. Bend forward at the same time you twist your body to throw the reverse Side Teep with your rear leg.

Things to remember: To practice the backward Teep, you must Teep with the kicking foot staying very close to the supporting leg as you chamber, in order for the Teep to be thrown straight. To throw the backward Teep straight, make sure your kicking foot passes by the other leg closely as it is chambered and thrown to the target.

Chapter 6 – The Art of Using Knees

The knee is the part of the body that connects the upper leg bones and lower leg bones. It has a patella (the knee cap) which is a concave, round bone that is very strong. It's the center between the upper and lower leg bones, which is supported by tendons, membrane, and muscle to keep the knee joint tight together. The muscles of the upper leg (quadriceps/hamstring) are large strong muscles. When you fold the knee, it's like you are merging all of the muscles of upper leg and lower leg with the knee cap. By folding the knee, these muscles and the knees joint tuck together, making the knee a strong weapon.

The knee is a short weapon. It's most effective when used at a close distance. For example, knees are effective when you are merged with the opponent inside of the clinch or thrown from a short distance from your opponent.

Targets for the knee are the **belly, chest, ribs,** and **side body**. The knee can be thrown to higher targets as well - **the arms, chin, face,** and **head**.

The knee can also be used to protect you from opponents' kicks to the body and legs by checking. This is because the combination of the knee and the muscles around it is very strong and can withstand a lot of impact, especially from kicks, if you can fold the knee to use it as a shield.

If you defend a kick with the knee, the lower leg of the person who threw the kick at you might actually get injured afterwards, because the knee is a more solid part of your bone structure to hit.

There are 5 types of Knee Strikes

1. Straight Knee
2. Flare Knee
3. Curve Knee
4. Flying Knee
5. Blocking Knee

Straight Knee

The Straight knee is a knee that is thrown fast and snappy, with the trajectory from the starting point straight to the target.

The target of the straight knee is the **belly** or the **sternum**.

How to do the Straight knee (from the Orthodox Stance):

1. When you throw the straight knee, twist the ball of the foot of the standing leg in order to send the force to the throwing knee.

2. Your body leans back to deliver the straight knee

3. The hand on the opposite side of the throwing knee covers your face and the arm tucks into the body

4. The hand on the same side of the throwing knee swings back, in the opposite direction of the throwing knee.

5. Once you hit the target, return to your stance.

6. Throw the straight knee from a short range from your opponent.

Remarks: Normally straight knees are used to hit the opponent without grabbing the neck of the opponent down. The most important thing to remember is the hand on the opposite side of the throwing knee must be at your eyebrow and the arm tucks in to the body. If you have grabbed the opponents' neck, you should grab with two hands. If you've grabbed the opponents' neck with two hands, make sure to tuck your elbows in towards one another as much as you can and tuck your chin to your chest or shoulders. This will make it difficult for your opponent to do anything back to you as deliver the straight knee.

Flare Knee

The Flare knee is similar to the straight knee. The differences between the straight knee and flare knee are as follows.

The target of the flare knee is **the lower part of the rib cage and the upper leg**.

1. The direction of the flare knee is not straight. If throwing the right flare knee, the direction the flare knee is thrown from right to left. If throwing the left flare knee, the direction of the flare knee is thrown from left to right.

2. When your opponent is approaching you straight on and you want to deliver a flare knee, you need to use 'Slant Step' to step to the side to deliver the Flare Knee.

    If you're throwing the left knee, use 'Slant Step (Right)'.

    If you're throwing the right knee, use 'Slant Step (Left)'.

Curve Knee

The Curve knee is thrown by lifting the knee up to the side and then curving it down by twisting the hips down in the direction of the knee.

The target is the **face, the side body,** and **the upper leg**.

This knee is thrown primarily from inside of the clinch. Jump into the curve knee to make it a heavier strike.

Flying Knee

The Flying Knee is similar to the straight knee in that you send it straight to the target, but instead of just stepping forward into the knee, you jump and send your body straight forward. Another version of the Flying Knee is where you jump straight upwards to reach the target.

The target is the **chin** or the **sternum**.

Blocking Knee

The Blocking Knee is thrown sort of like a half kick and half knee in that the knee is thrown like a kick with the leg parallel to the floor and the knee is folded with the calf tucked into the hamstring.

The benefit of this knee is that it is used as a way to prevent the opponent from throwing strikes at you by posting against the opponents' midsection with the shin.

The target is the **belly**, the **ribs**, or the **chest**.

Chapter 7 – The Art of Using Elbows

The Elbow is the part of the body that is the joint between the upper arm bone and lower arm bone. This part of the body is very strong and sharp. The elbow is a short weapon that's best when used in close distance fighting. Normally, when throwing elbows, you shouldn't tighten up your fist because it affects the sharpness of the elbow. There are 6 types of elbows.

1. Downward Hit Elbow – *'Sok Thee'*
2. Cut Elbow – *'Sok That'*
3. Up Elbow – *'Sok Nguad'*
4. Spear Elbow – *'Sok Poong'*
5. Tomahawk Elbow – *'Sok Gratoong'*
6. Reverse Elbow – *'Sok Glab'*

Downward Hit Elbow ('Sok Thee')

Downward Hit Elbow is an elbow that is thrown from the direction of up to down, passing by your face, similar to the short overhand. The key thing to remember is that the shoulder of the throwing arm tucks to the ear as you throw the Downward Hit Elbow.

The target of the Downward Hit elbow is the **eyes, temple, jaw, nose,** and **collar bone**.

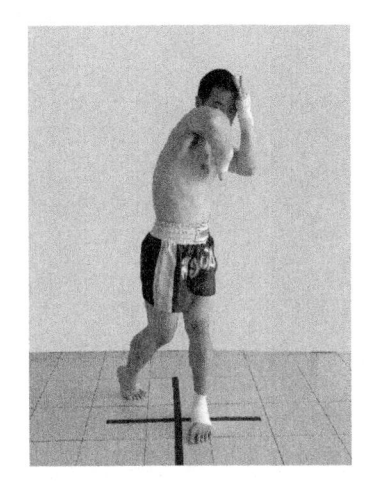

Downward Hit Elbow (*Sok Thee*)
Front View

Downward Hit Elbow (*Sok Thee*)
Side View

How to Hit with the Downward Hit Elbow (from the Orthodox Stance)

1. Fold the elbow joint of the throwing arm tightly, as much as can.

2. Swing the shoulders, with the shoulder of the throwing arm tucking towards the ear as the elbow is thrown from up to down.

3. Relax your hands, the index finger of the throwing arm swings to point down as you throw the elbow forward.

4. The ball of the foot on the same side of the throwing elbow twists according to the amount of force you are trying to generate with the elbow.

5. The hand on the opposite side of the throwing arm must stay at the eyebrow.

6. You can throw the elbow standing in place or stepping forward. It depends on the distance between you and your opponent.

7. This elbow can be thrown stepping forward or using 'Pivot Step', '1/4 Turn In', or '1/4 Turn Out' footwork.

Cut Elbow ('Sok Taht')

The Cut Elbow is an elbow that's thrown with the arm parallel to the floor, using the force from the ball of the foot as the pivot point. Send the force from the ball-of-the-foot to the leg, hip, shoulder and to the weapon.

The target of the Cut Elbow is the **eyes, temple, jaw, nose, outside ribs**, or the **lower rib cage**.

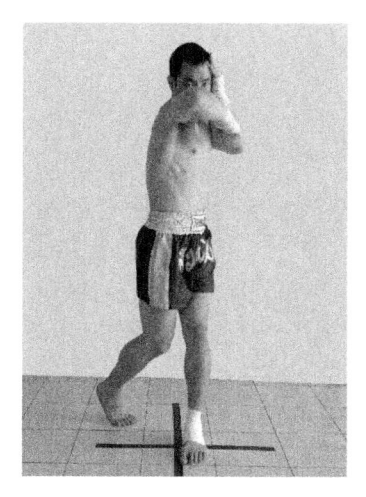

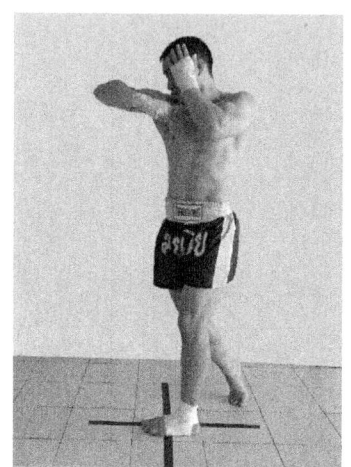

Cut Elbow (*Sok Taht*)
Front View

Cut Elbow (*Sok Taht*)
Side View

How to hit with the Cut Elbow

1. Fold the elbow joint of the throwing arm tightly, as much as can, with the palm of the hand face down

2. Use the ball of your foot as the pivot point

3. Swing your shoulder from the side to the front, parallel to the floor. Once you hit the target pull it back right away.

4. You can throw the cut elbow, in place, generating force by pivoting your foot, or you can step forward into it. It depends on the distance between you and your opponent.

5. The Cut elbow can be thrown standing in-place, stepping forward or using *Pivot Step*, *1/4 Turn In*, or *1/4 Turn Out* footwork.

Technique: To train throwing the cut elbow, practice hitting a target, landing with just the bony part of your elbow.

Up Elbow ('Sok Nguad')

The Up Elbow is thrown by sending the elbow from lower to higher. It's really similar to Short Uppercut. Flex the thrown elbow tightly at the point of contact, just like for the Downwards Hit Elbow and the Cut Elbow.

The target is the **sternum, chin, lower rib cage, chin, blood vessels surrounding the heart (chest)**, and **eyes**.

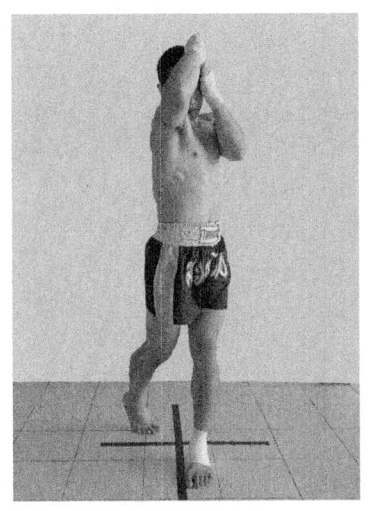

Up Elbow (*Sok Nguad*)
Front View

Up Elbow (*Sok Nguad*)
Side View

How to hit with the Rear Up Elbow: (From the Orthodox Stance):

1. Start by folding the throwing arm elbow at an acute angle (<90°)

2. The elbow travels from lower to higher. Use the pivot of the ball-of-your-foot as the generating force of the elbow. Send that force through the knee, hips shoulders, into the elbow.

3. When the elbow reaches the target, the back part of your throwing hand (the right hand) touches your left ear. The arm crosses the face to protect the face while throwing the elbow and to add more power to the weapon.

4. Lift the left palm up to protect yourself from opponents' potential incoming weapon.

5. The left arm tucks into your body.

6. You can throw the Up Elbow standing place or stepping forward to throw it. It depends on the distance between you and your opponent.

7. The Lead and Rear Up Elbow can be thrown standing in-place, using *Step Forward*. The Up Elbow can also be thrown using '1/8 Turn In' and 'Pivot Step' to throw the right Up Elbow.

8. An opportune time to throw the Up elbow is as your opponent tries to grab your arms or neck to clinch you up.

Spear Elbow (*'Sok Poong'*)

The Spear Elbow is thrown with your lead elbow straight to the target. To throw your Spear Elbow, point the tip of your elbow forward when you fold your elbow joint, with the upper arm parallel to the floor. The left hand touches the right ear and the palm of the right hand touches the palm of the left hand. This is to protect you from the opponents' attacks as you throw the elbow.

The target is the **eyes, nose** or the **sternum**.

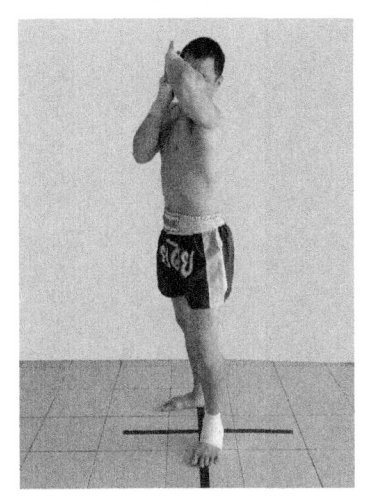

Spear Elbow (*Sok Poong*)
Front View

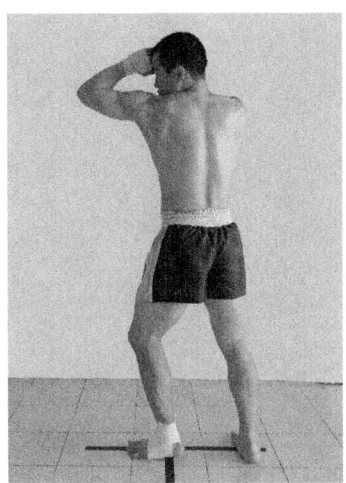

Spear Elbow (*Sok Poong*)
Side View

How to Hit with the Spear Elbow (From the Orthodox Stance):

1. Use the Spear Elbow as a way to hit your opponent with your lead elbow as they move toward you. You judge the incoming force of your opponent towards you. They could be stepping forward at you either to throw a punch, a knee, or try to clinch you up. As they step forward, you merge with the opponent, using *Step Forward* to reach the opponent with your Spear Elbow or '*Chawk*' and strike with the Spear Elbow simultaneously by using *1/8 Turn In (left)* to step to the inner angle of the opponent, ending with your body positioned 45° off the original centerline.

2. To make the elbow powerful and heavy, your lead foot touches the ground the same time the lead elbow touches the target.

3. The Spear Elbow using *1/8 Turn In (left)* can be used to defend the Jab. The Spear Elbow using *1/8 Turn In (right)* can be used to defend the Cross.

Tomahawk Elbow (*'Sok Gratoong'*)

To '*Gratoong*' in Thai means to stab downwards onto something. So, for Tomahawk Elbow, you raise your arm up to throw it straight down. Tomahawk Elbow can be thrown either on two feet or you can throw a jumping Tomahawk Elbow.

The target is the **skull, the artery to the lungs (chest), the collar bone,** and **the aorta (chest)**.

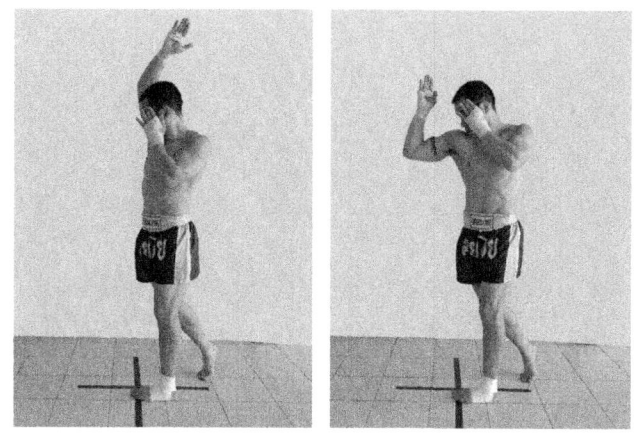

Tomahawk Elbow (*Sok Gratoong*)
Side View

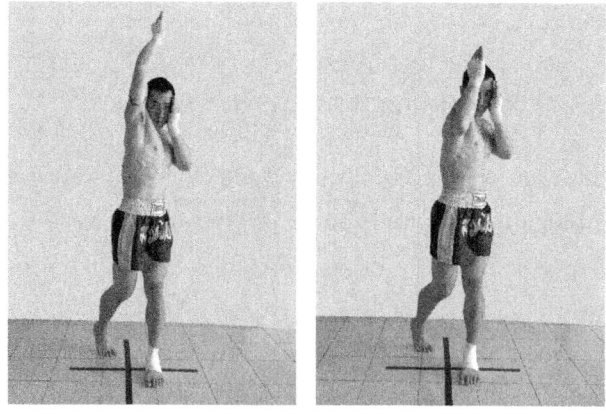

Tomahawk Elbow (*Sok Gratoong*)
Front View

How to throw the Tomahawk Elbow (from the Orthodox Stance):

1. Raise your throwing arm straight up

2. Jerk your shoulder down to throw the Tomahawk Elbow by folding your arm at an obtuse angle (>90°) and making the tip of your elbow touch the target.

3. Use your ball of the foot as the pivot point to help send the force from the foot to the knee, hips, shoulder and through the weapon.

4. Tomahawk Elbow can be used either defensively or for offense.

Technique: How you fold your arm to do this elbow is different from how you throw the previous elbows we've discussed. For this elbow, if you really fold your elbow tightly into an acute angle, just like for the Downward Hit Elbow, the part of the elbow that reaches the target won't be the tip of the elbow, but it will be the muscle on your arm. That's why when you throw Tomahawk Elbow, you need to throw it with the elbow folded at an obtuse angle.

Reverse Elbow ('Sok Glab')

The Reverse elbow is thrown by spinning your body so your back is facing the opponent, in order to throw the elbow to the opponent. The reverse elbow is thrown either parallel to your shoulders or from up to down.

The target of the reverse elbow is the **temple, jaw,** or **nose**.

How to hit with the Reverse Elbow:

1. The key to landing the reverse elbow is foot placement. You must place your foot at the correct position in relation to your opponent in order to create a pivot point to generate the power.

2. The spot that you position your pivot foot is directly in front of the opponents' lead foot. The distance from your foot and the opponents' foot is no more than the distance between your thumb and tip of your index finger. It can be closer than that.

3. After throwing the reverse elbow to the opponent, the elbow lands with your body posture straight.

4. The good thing about this elbow is that you can use it to defend against curved attacks such as the left hook, the right hook, and the high cut kick.

Technique: It's kind of hard to estimate the distance of the reverse elbow to the target, because as you turn your body, you cannot see the target. But what can help you with judging the distance correctly is using the position of your feet. The distance between your foot and your opponents' foot is approximately the distance between your thumb and tip of your index finger.

Remarks:

1. When you throw the reverse elbow, you are throwing the entire shoulder into the target, using your body weight.

2. When you throw the reverse elbow, you need to use your ball of the foot as the pivot point. In order to do this move correctly, you must train to spin your body backwards by stepping your feet while maintaining your balance.

3. To make your reverse elbow more efficient, keep your eyes on the tip of your elbow as you turn your back to the opponent all the way to when it reaches the target.

Chapter 8 – The Losing Cycle of Weapons

The 'Losing Cycle of Weapons', represents a way of thinking of how the weapons relate with one another, similar to the game 'Rock, Paper, Scissor'. *'Puncher, Kicker, Elbower, Kneer'* – the Losing Cycle of Weapons. The weapons in this cycle will defeat the weapon after it, but lose to the weapon which precedes it in the cycle.

The Losing Cycle Of Weapons

```
        Loses to          Loses to
                Puncher
        
    Kicker              Kneer
        
                Elbower
        Loses to          Loses to
```

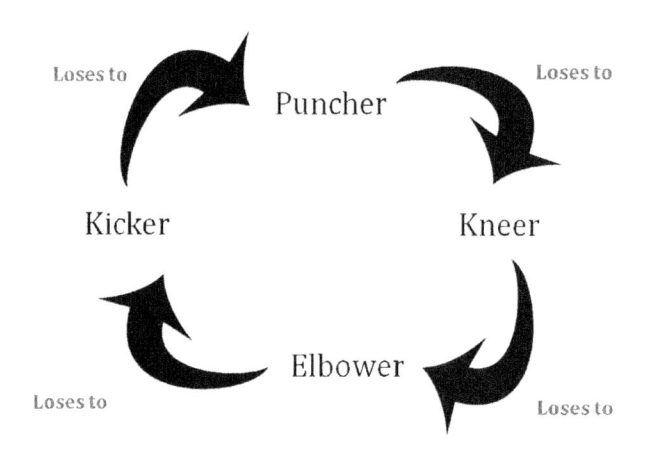

The Kicker loses to the Puncher. The Straight punches (Jab and the Cross) are effective weapons for stopping the Kick. Because the Jab and Cross are thrown straight to the target, they reach the target faster than the kick, which follows an angular trajectory to reach the target. To defeat the Kicker, the Puncher will move forward, overwhelming the Kicker with punches and not allowing him to set his feet to deliver his preferred weapon.

The Puncher loses to the Kneer. The Puncher is effective only if he has his arms free to throw his punches. The Kneer excels at grappling, trapping his opponents' arms and moving in to neutralize the Punchers' arms and neck before setting up his knee strikes. From this position, it would be difficult for the Puncher to throw an effective punch at the Kneer. With the upper body in firm control, the Kneer is in an advantageous position to deliver the knee to the Puncher.

The Kneer loses to the Elbower. The Kneer and Elbower are both adept at fighting at close range and inside of the clinch. One thing that the Kneer needs to be cautious of when engaging in grappling with an Elbower is getting elbowed while approaching to clinch. In order to clinch, the

Kneer must get both hands on the Elbower, forcing him to square up his shoulders to reach the Elbower with both arms, at the risk of getting elbowed. If the Kneer happens to secure the Clinch position, he still puts himself in danger when trying to throw his knee strike against the Elbower. The Kneer must lift his knee to throw his weapon. Lifting the knee temporarily puts the Kneer in a position where he can get hit with an elbow to the face or head by the Elbower.

The Elbower loses to the Kicker. The Elbower is adept at fighting at short range, and will lose to the kicker, who is adept at fighting at long range. In order to hit the Kicker, the Elbower has to get in close range to the Kicker. The Kicker, adept at using his *'Chawk Nawk'* footwork to keep the Elbower outside of arms range, will make it difficult for the Elbower to keep the game within arm's reach. In order to land the elbow, the Elbower needs to step into the Kickers kicking range. As the Elbower steps into range to throw his weapon, the Kicker will use his leg kicks to strike the lead leg.

'The Losing Cycle of Weapons' can serve the practitioner of Muay Thai as a base point for studying how to efficiently and effectively to use the weapons of Muay Thai. In reality, no fighter only throws just one weapon. The theory represents a model for how to think about the weapons of Muay Thai as they relate to one another. This cycle does not represent an absolute rule of how a fight will play out. Some skilled Kickers have been able to make fighting careers off of defeating heavy punchers.

In Chapter 3 (footwork), Chapter 4 (punches), Chapter 5 (kicks/teeps), Chapter 6 (knees), and Chapter 7 (elbows), we went over the basics of Muay Thai. These comprise the basics of Muay Thai, or what is known as *'Mae Mai Muay Thai'* or 'Basic Techniques of Muay Thai'. Before someone considers competing in Muay Thai, there grasp of *'Mae Mai Muay Thai'* must be legit.

In the following chapter, we will go over basic defense. Specifically, we will be going over the defensive techniques called *'Bid Bong':* the basic blocks, catches, parries, and techniques used to neutralize the incoming force of the opponent used to defend the 4 weapons of Muay Thai.

Chapter 9 – Basic Defense of Muay Thai (Bid Bong)

'*Bid Bong*' refers to the basic defensive techniques of Muay Thai used to block, catch, parry, or neutralize the incoming force of the attackers' weapon. '*Bid Bong*' is used to protect yourself from the attackers' weapon. The purpose is to reduce the force of the attack from very strong, to not as strong, without necessarily counter attacking. This is done primarily by using parts of your body that are stronger to protect those that are weaker. For example, using your arm (stronger) to shield your face (weaker).

Generally speaking, you shouldn't use the same block, catch, or parry technique to defend the same weapon more than two times in a row. One reason for this is because if you are using a stronger part of your body to shield a weaker part, the stronger part will weaken through repeated impact. So the stronger part will start to damage. Another reason you shouldn't use the same block, catch, or parry technique more than two times in a row, is to avoid becoming predictable to your opponent. If you use the same technique three times in a row, your opponent will use your predictable pattern of movement against you.

We will now go over '*Bid Bong*' - the basic blocks, catches, parries, and defensive techniques used to neutralize the incoming force of the 4 weapons of Muay Thai (punch, kick, knee, elbow).

Jab '*Bid Bong*'

1. Catch the Jab with the Palm of your Rear Hand.

Put your hand directly in front of your face to catch the Jab. If your opponent punches straight to your face, instead of hitting your face, it is going to hit your palm instead. If your opponent misses the target, the punch won't touch your face anyway.

One reason we use the rear hand to catch the punch instead of the lead hand is because the rear arm is tucked into your body, allowing you to absorb the force of the jab better. By catching with the rear hand, you are also able to keep your guard high on the left side, preventing you from getting countered by the opponents' cross.

To better absorb the force of the Jab, tense your rear arm and wrist tightly when you catch the Jab.

If the opponent throws the jab without stepping in, just catch the jab with your rear hand without stepping back. If the opponent steps forward into the jab, you can reduce the force of the jab by catching it using *Retreat* in order to reduce the force, stepping both feet back with the incoming force.

2. Catch the Jab with Your Lead Elbow

When your opponent punches straight to your face with the Jab, his fist will hit your folded elbow. If your opponent misses the target, the punch won't touch your face anyway.

3. Parry the Jab Inward with the Palm of Your Rear Hand

When parrying the Jab inward, parrying the top of the hand down and to the side will make the parry more effective.

Cross 'Bid Bong'

The Cross is a very powerful punch. So the 'Bid Bong' for Cross has to be executed with solidity and stability.

1. Catch the Cross with the Lead Elbow

2. Block the Cross with Your Arm

Block the Cross by folding your elbow and grabbing the side of your head. The tip of your elbow points forward and slightly inward, away from the cross. Twist your body slightly into the Cross in order for the fist to skim off your arm. This is different than technique #1, where you catch the opponents' fist directly on your lead elbow.

3. Parry the Cross with the Palm of Your Rear Hand

When parrying the Cross, parrying the top of the hand down and to the side will make it more effective.

Body Cross 'Bid Bong'

1. Parry the Body Cross –with– the palm of your hand or your lower arm

Use *Parry Mid-line* footwork to help.

1a. Parry Body Cross with *Parry Mid-line* to the Right

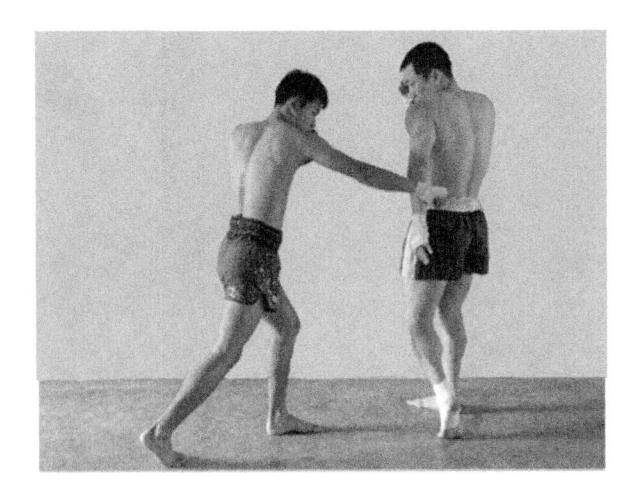

1b. Parry Body Cross with *Parry Mid-line* to the Left

Overhand Punch (Short and Long) *'Bid Bong'*

1. Block the Short Overhand with Your Arm

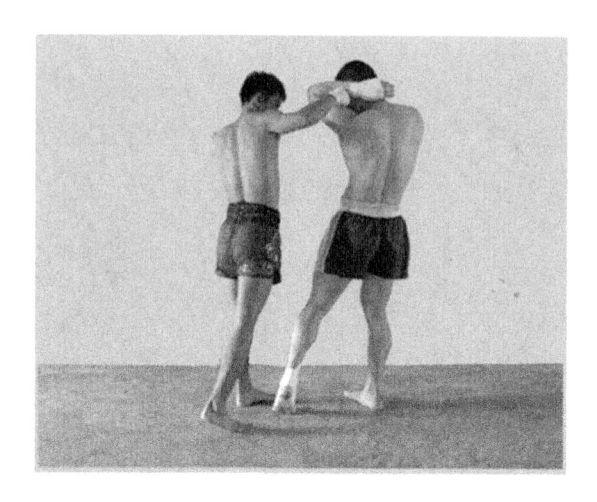

Fold your elbow and grab your ears.

2. Block the Long Overhand Punch with your Arm

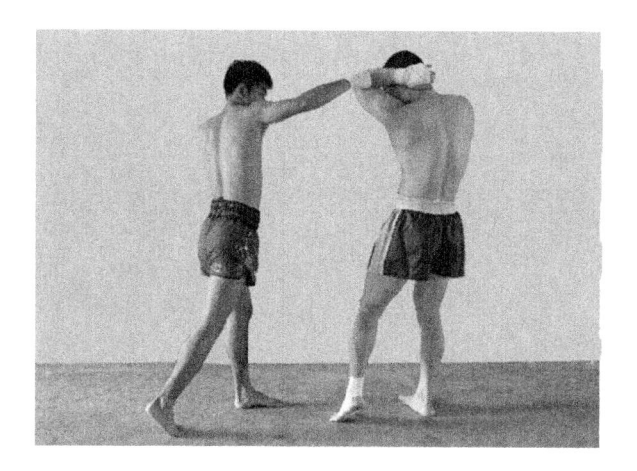

Fold your elbow and grab your ears.

3. Stop the Upper Arm of the Long Overhand Punch with Your Lower Arm

3a. Stop the Left Long Overhand Punch

To Stop the Left Long Overhand Punch use '*Slant Step (left)*' to parry the punch with your right lower arm

3b. Stop the Right Overhand Punch

To Stop the Right Long Overhand Punch use '*Slant Step (right)*' to parry the punch with your left lower arm

To reach the opponent's upper arm with your lower arm when he throws the long overhand, use '*Slant Step*'. The footwork you'll use depends on the side that the opponent is throwing the overhand from. The reason you want to stop their upper arm is because the force of the overhand punch is generated from the upper arm. So if you can stop the generator from moving, then you stop the punch.

Kick '*Bid Bong*'

1. Stop the Low Kick or High Kick by stepping Your Foot on the knee/upper leg. (opposite side)

Your opponent starts to kick with his left foot, use your left foot sole to step the foot to your opponents' leg. This method works both with an incoming low kick or incoming high kick.

If your attacker is throwing the left high kick to the body, land your left foot higher up on the left leg.

If the attacker is throwing the left low kick, land your left foot below the left knee.

If the attacker throws right kick, use your right foot and place it on the right leg.

2. Block the High Kick with Your Elbow

Use the area close to your elbow to stop the kick. The target is to catch the kick around the middle shin, ankle or foot. This technique has the potential to break the opponents' shin. For the Body Kick, use '_Slant Step_' to step slightly to the side away from the incoming force to catch the shin with your elbow.

3. Stop the High Kick with the palms of Your Hands to Brace the Upper Leg

When your opponent is kicking, the heaviness of the kick is generated from the upper part of the leg, so if you can step to the inner radius of the upper leg and push against it with the right rhythm, you will be able to stop the kick.

The heaviness of the kick will be reduced to the weight of just the lower leg and you will have evaded the kick. Use *1/4 Turn Out* footwork to execute this movement, moving in the direction away from the incoming force of the kick. (i.e. – if opponent throws the right body kick, use *1/4 Turn Out (right)* footwork) **

This technique is used for training purposes to teach the student how to get away from the kick while neutralizing its power. To turn it into a counter, instead of pushing the leg with the hands, use *1/4 Turn Out* footwork to throw your overhand punch

4. Block the Kick with your knee or upper shin

Use your knee or upper shin to check the high kick to the body. Start by lifting your knee straight up before curving it outward to catch the opponents' shin.

Use *Lift Knee* footwork.

Spinning Back Kick *Bid Bong*

1. Use your elbow to catch the opponents' calf muscle.

Step in, using *Slant Step* to step off the centerline and forward, slightly away from the incoming force of the spinning back kick. Angle your elbow outward to catch the back of the opponents' calf muscle.

2. Use the palms of your hand to push the back of your opponents' leg as he turns.

Use *Step Forward* to close the distance. Remember, when you *Step Forward* in Muay Thai, you must bring both feet forward.

3. Use the palms of your hand to push your opponents back as he turns.

As the opponent turns his back and he is beginning to kick backward, use *Step Forward* footwork to close distance and push his back with your palms.

Straight Teep *'Bid Bong'*

1. Parry the Straight Teep with your lower arm or palm of your hand (using *Parry Mid-line* footwork to help)

1a. Parry the Lead Teep (with *Parry Mid-line* to the Right)

1b. Parry the Rear Teep (with *Parry Mid-line* to the Left)

This technique is similar to the parry used for the Body Cross. Utilizing *Parry Mid-line* footwork with this technique will really break the rhythm of your opponent, opening him up for your counter-attack.

2. Block the Straight Teep with Your Knee

Use *Lift Knee*.

3. Block the Straight Teep by tucking your elbows to your body

Use this in the case, where you cannot parry the Teep or lift your knee to catch the Teep fast enough. Tuck your elbows into your body to absorb the Teep. Absorbing the Teep against the arms is better than just allowing the Teep to hit your chest or belly.

Side Teep 'Bid Bong'

1. For the Side Teep to Belly, you can use Straight Teep 'Bid Bong' #1-3.

1a. Parry the Side Teep,

Use *Parry Mid-line.*

Elbow 'Bid Bong'

1. For the 'Downward Hit Elbow', block the elbow with your arm (fold your elbow and grab your ears)

This block is similar to Overhand '*Bid Bong*' #1.

2. To '*Bid Bong*' the Tomahawk Elbow, <u>*Step Forward*</u> and use your lower arm to stop the opponents' upper arm.

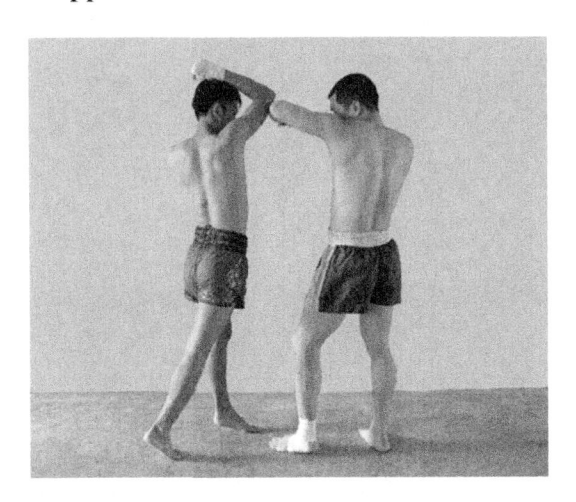

Remember to step both feet forward into the block.

3. Use your Elbow to Stop the Reverse Elbow.

3.1 Touch your Rear Elbow to the Attackers' Shoulder to Stop the Reverse Elbow.

3.2 Touch your Lead Elbow to the Opponents Shoulder to Stop the Reverse Elbow,

Use *Pivot Step (Left)* to execute this technique.

Knee *'Bid Bong'*

1. Use your elbows to Stop the opponents' knees.

2. Use your shin to block the opponents' knee.

Using Footwork to Evade the Opponents' Weapons

In addition to your '*Bid Bong*' techniques (your blocks, catches, parries, and defensive techniques) you can use your footwork to evade the attackers' weapons. For example, you can defend against the jab using just the basic footwork of Muay Thai.

Defending the Jab Using Footwork
(From the Orthodox Stance)

Evade the Jab using *Retreat*

Evade the Jab using *Diagonal Retreat (Right)*

Evade the Jab using *Diagonal Retreat (Left)*

Evade the Jab using *1/4 Turn Out (Right)*

In chapters 4, 5, 6, and 7 we went over the weapons of Muay Thai – punch, kick, knee and elbow. In this chapter, we went over the common basic defensive techniques for blocking, catching, and parrying the opponents' weapons – *'Bid Bong'*. We can also use our footwork to defend against the opponent by using it to evade.

In the following chapter, we will discuss the basic theory of rhythm in Muay Thai and how a Muay Thai fight can be broken down and thought of as a series of step sequences.

Actual fighting in Muay Thai is continuous flowing series of step sequences which occur between you and your opponent. Understanding rhythm, how to move with your opponents' rhythm, and how to break the opponents' rhythm is key to achieving a higher level of result from the application of your Muay Thai. To learn to defend yourself and attack effectively in Muay Thai, you need to learn how to continue the steps in the game beyond just executing step 1.

Chapter 10 - Basic Theory of Rhythm (in Muay Thai)

Rhythm (in Muay Thai) is a sequence of steps utilizing the techniques of Muay Thai from the beginning to the end of a particular fighting scenario. A particular rhythm between you and your opponent might be 1-step, 2-steps, 3-steps, 4, 5, 6…etc. Steps here does not mean just your footwork or how you throw your weapons. **The steps are a sequence of movements between you and your opponent – both of you.**

Throughout a particular rhythm where you may be attacking or defending, the movement of your body and your upper limbs needs to be correlated with your footwork, in order for you to maintain your balance and rhythm throughout the step sequence. The feet are always leading the body's movements – otherwise there will be a loss in balance, causing an interruption in your own rhythm.

The purpose of your rhythm is to achieve the following outcomes: 1) You don't get hurt and/or 2) you hurt or (KO) the opponent.

Counting the Steps in a Fighting Rhythm.

Start to count the steps of a particular fighting scenario, starting from 'Step 1', followed by 'Step 2, 3, 4, … until the end of the rhythm.

What happens at 'Step 1' on both sides? It could be anything.

Example 1

You: Jab (Step 1 for you)

Opponent: Steps Forward with 'Shooting Forward' Elbow (Step 1 for him also)

If that elbow hits you, this rhythm ends at Step 1. Your opponent wins this exchange.

Example 2

You: Jab (Step 1 for you)

Opponent: Kick (Step 1 for him)

Say he misses it.

You: Kick to the Head (Step 2 for you)

Opponent: Fixing his footwork (Step 2 for him)

If your kick hits him nice, then this rhythm ends at Step 2. You're in control of this game. But if your kick didn't hit, step 3 will happen and continue to Step 4, 5 … or the rhythm might just end at Step 3 if you can end the game with a KO.

As the fighter, your instinct should be

"I must touch the target first. It doesn't matter who initiates Step 1."

Basic Theory of Rhythm for Offense

Offensive combinations are used to tactically attack and mislead the opponent.

One-Step Offense (*'Mai Rook 'Neung'-Jung Wa'*) – Count One Step, Done. This kind of offense is easy to defend.

Two-Step Offense (*'Mai Rook 'Song'-Jung Wa'*) - The opening attack is a bluff to make the opponent off-balanced or reveal vulnerabilities. The second attack is performed with real execution and done immediately after the first attack. If your opponent gets hit right on the correct spot, you finish the game with a KO. If he can defend himself after the Two-Steps, you can continue it to Steps 3, 4...etc.

Three-Step Offense (*'Mai Rook 'Saam'-Jung Wa'*) – You do two opening attacks, then throw a heavy weapon, OR this is a continuation from a 'Two-Step Offense'.

Four-Step Offense – **and 5, 6, 7, 8**….END.

If your opponent has been hurt by your offensive combination and can't continue defending, you can try to finish the game with a KO shot. If the opponent can still defend himself or is attacking you, you continue defending yourself until you can get the game back from him. The instinct of the fighter is *"Always put yourself in the advantageous position. Always. You must feel that you own the game."*

Patterns of attack in your offensive combinations are used to maximize your chance of landing the shot. Some offensive combinations are thrown switching up the direction of attack from step to step. Some of these shots may be partial and not utilize the whole force of the attack, to spare control and speed for the subsequent attack.

Common Patterns of Attack for Offensive Rhythms

- attacking to all levels of the body - High, Middle, Low

- attacks coming from the left and then from the right, and vice versa

- attacks shooting straight-in (i.e. – Jab) followed by an attack which is thrown angularly (i.e. – roundhouse kick)

- a double attack in sequence to the same target

These tactics are to confuse the opponent and increase the probability of landing the shot. Whereas the previous strikes in the combination may be bluffs, the final step in the offensive combination is thrown with the entire body weight, with the intention of 'Game Over'.

Basic Theory of Rhythm for Defense

'Mai Rup' refers to the Art of Defense as it applies to Muay Thai. The word, defense, here is used in the sense of counter-attacking, using your attackers' attack as an opportunity to hit them back.

Muay Thai Defense Strategy - At a Glance

Block, Catch, Parry, to Neutralize the Incoming Force (*'Bid Bong'*) - Collect the attackers weapons using *'Bid Bong'* in this sense means you are collecting the patterns or "style" the attacker uses to attack, studying his style of fighting.

Counter-Attacking (*'Gae-Awoot'*) Using your *'Bid Bong'* techniques, you study the attackers' fighting style, collect the patterns of the attacker, studying his fighting style. From this, you come up with how you are going to do something back.

Does your attacker expose his chin when he throws the kick? Is the attacker slow to return his hands to his face after throwing his punches? Use your eyes to study the attacker as you use your *'Bid Bong'* to defend. From that, you come up with how you are going to do something back.

Step 1 vs. Step 2 Counter-attacks

From the perspective of rhythm, there are two types of counter-attack.

Step 1 Counter-Attack (*'Ching Chok'*) – Your attacker engages by establishing an opening attack on step 1. You have no intention of being offensive, but you see the opening on your attacker. You throw the weapon at the same time the attacker does and land the shot at the same step.

Step 2 Counter-Attack (*'Suan'*) – During your attackers' offensive combination, you use your *'Bid Bong'* to defend on Step 1 and on Step 2, quickly throw your weapon to your target to reach it before your attacker reaches his target. For example, you might use your *'Bid Bong'* on the second strike in a combination and hit the attacker before he can reach his target for the third strike in the combination.

Step 1 Counter-Attacks and Step 2 Counter-Attacks are both executed with the mindset "*I'm going to land my shot first*".

Offensive Rhythm vs. Defensive Rhythm

Offensive rhythm is about speed, being deceptive, even cocky at times, as a way to create an opening to land your heavy weapon. We'll be discussing that further later in this book in Chapter 11 – 'The Art of Muay Thai Offense', and the Additional Offensive Combinations in the Addendum.

The rhythm of Defense (and Counter-attacking) is about timing. Specifically, the timing is executing the proper footwork for your counterattack, at the same time the attacker throws his weapon at you. In Chapter 13 – 'The Art of Muay Thai Defense', we will be going over the higher level of Muay Thai, counter attacking techniques. This chapter will break down the higher level counter-attack techniques by showing you how the perfect execution of them is based on footwork timing. Also, there are Additional Defensive Techniques in the Addendum.

Training the Eyes for the Rhythm of Fighting

Although this is a book about footwork, eyes are an important part of the body for the Muay Thai fighter to train.

When you're defending and counter-attacking, the eyes are important for being able to sense the opponents' rhythm, judging distance between you and the attacker, and ensuring that your counter-attack reaches the target.

When you're attacking, the eyes are important for being able to see the openings in your opponents' defense, judging distance between you and the opponent, so that the weapons you select to use in your combinations are thrown from a distance at which they are effective. (i.e. – after landing your jab, you can sense that you are too far away to have a chance to land your elbow next, you might follow up instead with a kick or another punch.)

It takes time to develop eyes which are developed enough to keep up with the pace of an actual fight. With an opponent that is constantly moving and shifting distance away from you, at first it becomes difficult to judge the appropriate range at which your attacks are effective. As you become more adept at identifying the correct range to throw your strikes using your eyes, you will be able to better reach to the target with your footwork.

The rhythm of actual fighting is very fast. This is why it's important to start slowly to build the proper coordination between your eyes and your feet. As you train Muay Thai, hitting pads, hitting the bag, shadowboxing – it's important to remember the actual target you are trying to hit.

As you train Muay Thai – hitting the pads, hitting the bag, shadowboxing - always train with your eyes, seeing with your imagination, (one) the target and (two) your weapons of fist, foot, knee, and elbow smashing through the target. This will train your subconscious mind and improve your ability to see and reach the target while developing a sense of distance for throwing you're your weapons.

Chapter 11 – The Art of Muay Thai Offense (Mai Rook)

You use your basic weapons in combination, your *'Mae Mai Muay Thai'*, to create your offense (*'Mai Rook'*). Offense is about being tricky, cocky, fast with your weapons as well as being able to throw your weapons with power when you see the open shot. .

Opening Weapons for Offense

Normally, the opening weapon for your offense utilizes weapons which are long range, fast, and concise. Normally, the characteristics of a good opening weapon are 1) you maintain a strong base after throwing the weapon 2) it's fast and 3) it's a long distance weapon. Common Muay Thai techniques that have these 3 properties include the jab, straight Teep, diagonal kick, straight kick, and Side Teep,

After the opening weapon, you can use your other weapons to continue your combination. One determining factor of what type of weapon you will use is distance. If the opponent is far after your opening weapon lands, you might continue with another long distance weapon. If the opponent is a short distance away after your opening weapon lands, you would use a short range weapon. Ultimately, the weapon you choose to use as your follow up will depend on the particular fighting scenario.

Landing Your Weapons Heavy vs. Bluffs

When throwing your offensive combinations, all of your shots can be heavy weapons or they can be all bluffs, or a combination of heavy weapons with bluffs.

When throwing your bluffs, throw fast and snappy and don't use all your body weight to go in. Save some of that weight to balance yourself in order to throw your heavy weapon on a next step. When throwing your heavy weapon, the one that you intend to do damage with, send all of your body weight through the target.

To land your heavy weapon, you often need to set it up with your offensive combinations When practicing your offensive combinations, practice with a rhythm in which you are positioning yourself to throw the heavy weapon in that combination, with all of your body weight.

At first, you might just practicing your two-step or three-step combinations as pre-set combinations that you practice (reference Addendum – Mai Rook for examples of 2-Step, 3-

Step, 4-step, 5-step, and 6-step combinations). There is no end to the number of possible offensive combinations that you could use against your opponent. The important thing is you are accurate with your combinations and that you are able to keep continuing your combinations after the opening weapon.

The combinations you can put together for Offense are endless. Learning to use all of your '*Mae Mai Muay Thai*' and combining them in various ways allows you to create your own combinations once you are skilled enough.

As a starting point for learning to throw your offensive combinations, start simple. For example, start by learning how to open high and then attack low, which will force your opponent to have to block high and then block low. If you throw two high attacks in a row, or two low attacks in a row, it's going to be easier for your opponent to defend.

Your Offensive combinations can work efficiently if you have the footwork skills and know how to shift your weight with the right speed. It all has to come together. By integrating the footwork, weight shift, and speed, your body will not tense up as you execute your offense. When you throw your weapons, only certain parts of your body should stay tense.

To learn how to throw your weapons with more of your body weight, as you train, be aware of the following:

1. How your weight should be shifting in your combinations (i.e. - from left foot to right foot, right foot to left foot)
2. Where the balls of your feet are (including distance from the opponent)
3. The Target

Again, there are nearly an endless number of offensive combinations. Which one to use depends on the fighting scenario and what you see as your opening.

In the following chapter, we will go over some basic history of Muay Thai and how the techniques of Muay Thai were passed down from generation. This will give you a context for our chapter on 'The Art of Muay Thai Defense'.

Chapter 12 - The History of Muay Thai

Muay Thai 'Boran' as an Art of War

Muay Thai 'Boran', is the ancient form of the sport we know as Muay Thai. The techniques of Muay Thai evolved from Muay Thai 'Boran', which had its application on the battlefields of South East Asia. 'Boran' means 'Ancient'. 'Muay' means 'Boxing'. And so Muay Thai Boran literally translates to Ancient Thai Boxing.

Muay Thai was turned into a ring sport officially in 1930, with standard rules, regulations, and weight classes based on the Marquess of Queensberry rules, employed for Western Boxing matches.

Today, Muay Thai (or Thai Boxing) is practiced all around the globe. Some people are drawn to Muay Thai by their interest in combat sports. Some are purely interested in the self-defense application of the art. Others train to develop a strong physical body, self-discipline, and inner strength.

Today, Muay Thai has gain the most attention and has been adapted into other fighting styles such as you'll see in MMA, due to the simple fact that it is ruthlessly effective martial art for Stand-up Striking.

In Thailand, Muay Thai is the national sport. The very best Muay Thai fighters compete regularly as prize fighters, making income for their family inside of the ring.

The techniques of Muay Thai were passed down from generation to generation within the Kingdom of Siam from teacher to student as wars were waged between Thailand and its' neighboring countries.

And so, the Muay Thai we know today, has its' roots in time-tested techniques which have their origins in actual martial fighting.

Muay Thai is referred to as 'The Art of 8 Limbs' – Two fists, Two feet, Two knees, and Two elbows. Through training of the techniques of Muay Thai, a practitioner of Muay Thai forges these 8 limbs into literal weapons.

The knuckles of the fist mimic small daggers. The elbows would be used as the head of a hammer. The knees would be used to stab into the opponent. The shins used as a blade of an axe for cutting the opponent down with kicks.

The Legacy of Nai-Kanom Tom

There is no longer an accurate record of the exact origins of Muay Thai. The original records containing that information were ransacked and destroyed by the Burmese army a long time ago. Today, the Thai's recognize Nai-Kanom Tom, a Thai soldier from the 18th century as the 'Father of Muay Thai'.

Nai-Kanom Tom, was captured by the Burmese as a prisoner of war. He was sent to be a gladiator, fighting other Burmese soldiers as a way to entertain the king. The soldier demonstrated the power of his country's martial art through defeating 10 of the Burmese kings very best soldiers, one after another. The king was so impressed by his performance, he remarked

"Every part of this Siamese is Blessed with Venom"

Then granted him his freedom. The date was March 17th 1774. And so Nai-Kanom Tom is known to be 'The Father of Muay Thai'. In remembrance, the people of Thailand and the Muay Thai community around the world acknowledge March 17th as Muay Thai Day, in remembrance of Nai-Kanom Tom.

The Culture of Thai People and Muay Thai

If you watch a kickboxing match between a Thai fighter and a Burmese or Cambodian kickboxer, the punches, elbows, knees, and kicks look very similar. Stylistically, the martial arts of Pradal Serey (Burma), Lethwei (Cambodia) and Muay Thai (Thailand) look very similar.

In regards to style, what makes Muay Thai Boran uniquely something of the Thai people is the set of higher level techniques of self-defense, known as 'Look Mai Muay Thai'. Whereas 'Mae Mai Muay Thai' represents the basic weapons and footwork, 'Look Mai Muay Thai' is the combination of those Mae Mai movements into more complex self-defense tactics.

'Look Mai Muay Thai' techniques were elegantly named by skillful Kru Muay's (Muay Thai Teachers) in a way which allowed them to effectively teach the art to their students through linking the techniques to common cultural aspects of the Thai people themselves. You have to remember that these techniques evolved generations ago, before the advent of the internet and efficient forms of public broadcasting.

The names of the Muay Thai techniques, including the 'Look Mai' Muay Thai' techniques that we will be going over in the following chapter, derive their names from 3 cultural aspects of the Thai people.

1. The 'Ramakien' (The Thai adaptation of a hugely popular Hindi Folk Tale – 'Ramayana'). Every Thai child grows up learning this story and is enmeshed in the Thai culture. Many of the advanced techniques of Muay Thai make reference to mythical characters from the story such as Arawan, a 3-headed elephant, or Hanuman, god-king of the apes.

2. The Observance of the Fighting Styles of Animals. For example, the Muay Thai kick would be compared to the way an elephant swings its' trunk to defend itself or how it attacks when it's angry.

3. The Everyday Life and Activities of Thai People. (a.k.a. – using a mortar and pestle to grind spices)

Chapter 13 – The Art of Muay Thai Defense

Mai Rup – The mechanism of mixing or blending the basic use of fists, feet, knees, elbows, and footwork - in order to '*Bid Bong*', get away, evade, and defend weapons from your opponent, in the way of the Art of 8 Limbs. The Counter-Attack techniques in this chapter represent some of the higher level techniques of Muay Thai.

In order for learners of Muay Thai to be able use '*Mai Rup*', they need to have a strong base in their '*Mae Mai Muay Thai*' (Basic Strikes and Footwork), '*Bid Bong*'(Block, Parry, Catch, Evade with Footwork), and '*Mai Rook*'(Offensive Combinations). To develop skill in '*Mai Rup*', which is counter attacking, they need to train until they have skills, until they own it. Through learning the footwork correctly, they will have rhythm, speed, accuracy, form, and sharpness in their basic punches, kicks, knees, and elbows.

Since Muay Thai in the ancient times wasn't a sport, all of the weapons that were created were aimed to defeat the opponent quickly.

Now, Muay Thai has become a sport. So there are rules, standards, and regulations in order to control the competition. Certain dangerous techniques that were a part of the original Muay Thai Boran have been prohibited from being used in the ring. If you want to use these prohibited techniques, use it to defend yourself in real life.

Please remember that when you train Muay Thai, you are preserving the Art. When Thai people fight to defend themselves, they don't use this Art as a way to bully anybody or show off. This is what all great teachers from every gym in the country of Thailand do not want to see.

Note: *The 24 Counter-Attack Techniques presented in this chapter have corresponding videos which have been uploaded to Youtube, which demonstrate these techniques. The photo's here are taken from those videos. To see the full technique, just go to the Youtube Channel Playlist.*

How to Access the Videos

1. Go to www.youtube.com
2. Search 'Muay Thai: The Footwork – Counterattacks'
3. Scroll down until you see the playlist (by Mastermind Muay Thai)

Web Address:

https://www.youtube.com/watch?v=iQVkM3HuJwg&list=PLvOG3_uiRS7W2IBhOcFQFwUFXB4LvaqEz

I'd like to say thanks to Ajarn Sukchai at the Physical Institute of Lampang, Thailand for permission to use these videos.

Razor Toothed Fish
('Salab Fun Bla')
Defend the Jab by Catching and Breaking the Elbow Joint

Attacker: Step in and throw the Jab to the Face.

Defender: Use *1/4 Turn Out (right)*, using your left hand to hook around the lower arm of the Attackers' jab. As the right foot lands, your right arm or palm pushes against the attackers' upper arm, right above the elbow.

The target is the **elbow joint of the Jabbing arm**.

Remarks: If your attacker throws the cross, just go to the opposite side using *1/4 Turn Out (left)*.

Break into the Birdie's Nest
('Baksa Waeg Rung')
Defend the Jab –with– Spear Elbow

Attacker: Step in and throw the Jab to the Face.

Defender: Use '1/8 Turn In (left)' with the Spear Elbow. To form the spear elbow, make an acute angle with your left elbow, with the left upper arm parallel to the floor. The back of your left hand touches the right side of your face. The right hand touches the left hand. The right arm tucks into your body. The tip of your left elbow goes straight to where the blood vessels connect to the **heart (aorta)** or to the **eyes of the attacker**.

The Javanese Lashes His Spear
('*Chawa Sod Hok*')
Defend Jab –with– Cut Elbow

Attacker: Step in and throw the Jab to the Face.

Defender: Use *1/4 Turn Out (right)* with Right Cut Elbow to step outside of the Jab and deliver the Right Cut Elbow to the **Left Side Shoulder Blade**. The right foot touches the ground the same time the right elbow hits the target.

Remarks: If the attacker steps in to throw the Cross, just do the opposite, using *1/4 Turn Out (left)*.

Enao Stabs With His Daggar
('Enao Tang Grit')
Defend Jab –with– Spear Elbow

Attacker: Step in and throw the Jab to the Face.

Defender: Use '1/8 Turn In (left)' with Left Spear Elbow. To form the spear elbow, make an acute angle with your left elbow, with the left upper arm parallel to the floor. The back of your left hand touches the right side of your face. The right hand touches the left hand. The right arm tucks into your body. The tip of your left elbow goes straight to the attackers **face**.

Remarks: If the attacker steps in to throw the Cross, just do the opposite, using *1/8 Turn In (right)*.

Prop up Mount Meru
('Yok Kao Pra Sumain')
Defend Jab –with– Rear Short Uppercut

Attacker: Step in and throw the Jab to the Face.

Defender: Use *Slant Step (Left)*, bending your knees as you step to the inner angle of the opponent. Twist your body and throw your 'Rear Short Uppercut' to the attackers' **chin**. After you land the strike, pull the right hand back, right back into your stance.

Priest bears large Winter Melon
('Tha Tain Kum Fug')
Defend Jab –with– Lead Short Uppercut

Attacker:

Step 1: Step in and throw the Jab to the Face.

Defender:

Step 1: Use *Slant Step (left)*, twisting your body forward with your right elbow. The right elbow is bent and the fingertips should be touching your ears. The tip of your right elbow points to the attackers' left upper arm.

Step 2: Twist the body and throw 'Lead Short Uppercut' to the attackers **chin** by using the **Left** foot as the Pivot point to generate the force.

Douse the Luminaries
('Dub Chawala')
Defend Jab –with– Jab

Attacker: Step in and throw the Jab to the Face.

Defender: Use *1/4 Turn Out (left)* to Jump with the Jab, hitting the Attackers' **face**.

The Mon temporarily bears the Foundation
('*Mon Yan Lak*')
Defend Jab –with– Jumping Side Teep

Attacker: Step in and throw the Jab to the Face.

Defender: Use *'Move Feet Around a Circle (to the left)'* to jump left into the Side Teep. Use the right foot as the base to jump clockwise at the same time you send your left leg towards the attacker's left side body. Land with heel or the sole of the foot. The target is the **chest** or **belly**. Your base foot, (the right foot) will point to the opposite direction of the target.

Pierce with a Sharp Edged Tool
('Buk Look Toy')
Defend High Kick –with– Up Elbow

<u>Attacker:</u> Steps forward to throw kick to defender's lower left rib.

<u>Defender:</u> Use *1/4 Turn Out (right)* with the Rear Up Elbow to hit the attackers' **shin**.

Crocodile thrashes its' Tail
(*'Jarake Faht Haang'*)
When your Attacker evades your kick, defend –with– Spinning Back Kick

Defender:

Step 1: Defender initiates by throwing Left High Kick to Attacker. The kick misses the target

Step 2: Off of the missed Left kick, land your left foot slightly over the centerline using *1/4 Turn In (left)* footwork to twist the body through the centerline to swing the right leg up. Land with the heel or just above the heel to slap down onto the attackers' **neck**.

Attacker:

Step 1: Attacker Steps back to evade Defenders' Left High Kick

Step 2: Attacker Steps forward to approach Defender to counter-attack and gets hit with the Spinning Heel Kick on the neck.

Break the Elephant's Trunk
('Hak Nguong Aiyara')
Defend High Kick by catching ankle and hitting leg –with– Tomahawk Elbow

Attacker: Steps in and throws the right high kick to the defender's lower left ribs

Defender: Use *1/4 Turn Out (right)* and hook your left arm under the attackers' ankle (turn your fist up). At the same time, twist the body and throw Right Tomahawk Elbow to the attackers' **quadriceps muscle.**

Remarks: If the attacker throws the **left** kick, do the opposite, using *1/4 Turn Out (left)* (at the same time the Attacker throws the left high kick).

Dragon Twists its' Tail
(*'Naka Bid Haang'*)
Defend Lead Straight Teep by catching Teep, twisting ankle, and hitting calf muscle –with– knee

Attacker: Step the Right foot forward to throw the lead Teep to the defenders' belly.

Defender: Use *Retreat* (as the Teep approaches the belly) and raise the palm of the left hand under the attackers' left foot, with the palm upward. Pull the left hand back to hook the ankle with the palm of your hand. Right hand grabs the attackers' ball of the foot. Raise the lead arm up and twist the attackers' ball of the foot down and clockwise. Throw the rear knee to the attackers' **calf muscle**.

Wii-roon-Hoak Returns
(*'Wii-Roon Hoak Glab'*)
Defend Low Kick –with– Heel Teep to Kicking Leg

Attacker: Throw the left kick to the defender's rear upper leg.

Defender: Use *Switch Stance Forward* footwork, bringing your rear foot forward narrowly and using your right heel to step on the attackers' left **quadriceps muscle** (at the same time the Attacker throws the left low kick).

Break Arawan's Neck
('Hak Kaw Arawan')
Defend Jab by Grabbing the Neck and Hitting –with– Knee

Attacker: Step in and throw the Jab to the Face.

Defender: Use *Slant Step (left)* and grab the back of the attacker's neck with both hands. Pull down to bend the attacker's spine down and then throw the left flare knee to the attackers' **lower ribs**.

Remarks: If the attacker steps in and throws the cross, do the opposite, using *Slant Step (right)*.

Giant Demon King rolls the Realm of the Humans
(*'He-Run Muan Pandin'*)
Defend High Kick –with– Reverse Elbow

Attacker: Step forward with the rear foot and throw the lead kick to the attackers' neck

Defender: Use *1/4 Turn In (left)* to step your lead foot close to the lead foot of the attacker. Your *1/4 Turn In (left)* should position you inside the inner radius of your attackers' upper leg (the kicking leg). Using the momentum of your footwork, spin your body to throw the reverse elbow to the attackers' **face**.

Remarks: The direction of the elbow has to be up and then down to split the guard. If you bring the elbow straight across, you might hit the attackers guard. To make the elbow heavier, turn your shoulders through to send the force down onto the target. Notice how the feet are positioned close as you land the Reverse Elbow.

'Tai Yuan' Casting Net for Fish
(*'Yuan Taud Hae'*)
Defend Lead Straight Teep –with– Straight Kick to Achilles Tendon

Attacker: Step your rear foot forward and throw the lead Teep to the knee

Defender: Use *Diagonal Retreat (Right)* to quickly evade the Teep and throw rear straight kick to the Attackers' Left **Achilles Tendon** as the attackers' foot is dropping towards the floor after the missed low Teep.

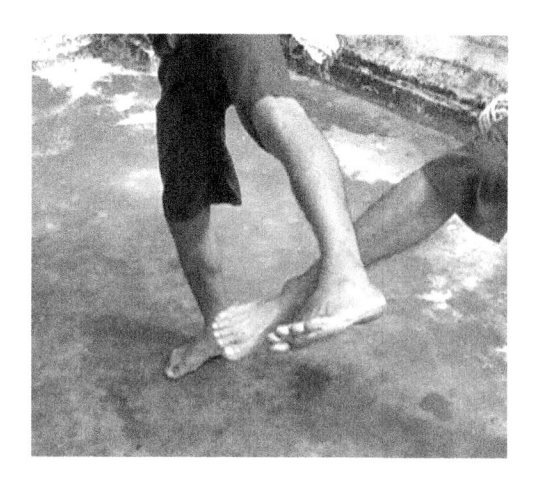

Slice a Squash into Thin Pieces
(*'Faan Look Buab'*)
Defend Jab –with– Up Elbow

Attacker:

Step 1: Step in and throw the Jab to the Face.

Defender:

Step 1: Use *Slant Step (left)*, twisting your body forward with your right elbow. The right elbow is bent and the fingertips should be touching your ears. The tip of your right elbow points to the attackers' left upper arm.

Step 2: Twist the body, throw left Up Elbow to the **chin**. Use the **left** foot as the pivot point to send the force.

Old Monk Sweeps the Courtyard with a Broom
(*'Tain Gwaad Laan'*)
Defend Lead Straight Teep –with– Rear Low Cut Kick

Attacker:

Step 1: Step forward with the right foot to throw the left Teep to the defenders' belly

Defender:

Step 1: Use *Parry Mid-line* to the Right, using the left wrist to catch the attackers' left foot.

Step 2: Step the left foot at the same time that you drop the body down. Throw the right kick to the attackers' right ankle (Achilles Tendon).

Break the Swans Wing
('Hong Beek Hak')
Defend the Cross —with— Downward Hit Elbow

Attacker: Step in and throws the cross to the Defenders' Face.

Defender: Use *1/4 Turn In (right)* with Downward Hit Elbow to evade the cross and deliver the Hit Elbow to the **collarbone**. You can also use Tomahawk Elbow to perform this technique.

Hermit grinds Medicine
('Rhu-see Boad-ya')
Defend Jab –with– Tomahawk Elbow

Attacker:

Step 1: Step in and throw the Jab to the Face.

Defender:

Step 1: Use *Diagonal Retreat (Right)*, using the lead arm to deflect the Jab.

Step 2: Step your **left** foot towards the attacker, with your left arm still in contact with the attacker's left arm from the deflection. As you step forward with your **left** foot, use your left hand to grab the attackers' left shoulder and prop your body up to throw Tomahawk Elbow to the **top of the head**.

Push Against a Pole, Diagonally
('Ta-yae Kum Sao')
Defend High Kick –with– Teep to the Supporting Leg

Attacker: Step the right foot forward and throw left kick to the neck of the defender.

Defender: Use *Slant Step (left)* twisting your body to the left and lifting your right foot to throw the Side Teep to the upper part of the supporting leg, **above the knee joint**. Land with the heel.

Lion Crosses a Creek
('Grai-Shon Kham Huay')
Defend High Kick –with– Low Cut Kick

Attacker: Step the right foot forward and throw the left kick to the defenders' neck.

Defender: Use *Slant Step (left)* bowing your upper body down to the left, shooting your right foot straight to your attacker's right ankle, in the **Achilles Tendon** area

Tattoo a Garland, on the Chest
('Suk Puang Malai')
Defend Jab –with– Tomahawk Elbow

Attacker:

Step 1: Step in and throw the Jab to the Face.

Defender:

Step 1: Use *Slant Step (left)*, twisting your body forward with your right elbow. The right elbow is bent and the fingertips should be touching your ears. The tip of your right elbow points to the attackers' left upper arm.

Step 2: Twist your body, lift the left elbow up, and twist your shoulders to throw the left Tomahawk Elbow to the chest, to the **blood vessel around the heart (aorta)**.

Arawan Swings its' Tusks
('Arawan Soei Ngaa')
Defend Jab –with– Rear Uppercut

Attacker:

Step 1: Step in and throw the Jab to the Face.

Defender:

Step 1: Use *Slant Step (right)*, using the lead arm to deflect the Jab.

Step 2: Step toward the attacker with your left foot and, at the same time, twist your body forward to throw the rear uppercut to the attackers' chin.

Remarks: To hit the target for this technique, you are throwing the Rear Uppercut underneath the attackers' arm.

Chapter 14 – Learning to Fight From Both Stances

Up to this point, this book was written from the context of the practitioner training from the Orthodox Stance. In order to maximize your ability to utilize the Art of 8 Limbs, it is important for you to learn how to use your footwork, throw your weapons, do *'Bid Bong'*, perform your defense *('Mai Rup')*, and your offense (*'Mai Rook'*) from both your Southpaw Stance and Orthodox Stance.

Being able to fight from both stances means that you can decide which fighting angle you want to fight your opponent at. For example, say you only know how to fight from the Orthodox Stance and are used to training against other Orthodox Stance fighters. If your opponent fights from the Southpaw Stance and is very strong at fighting Orthodox Stance fighters, he will have an advantage over you. If you learn to fight equally well from both the left and the Orthodox Stances, you can decide how you want to fight your opponent.

Being able to fight equally from both stances takes a lot of training.

The following exercises are the starting point for learning how to fight equally well on both sides.

Footwork Exercise for Developing Your Stance

Straight Punch Forward from Square Stance : (Exercise) This exercise is meant to improve the correlation of your hands with your footwork. The proper correlation of your hands and feet is important for all aspects of Muay Thai, including executing your offensive combinations with good rhythm, feeling natural and ready in your stance, '*Bid Bong*'(blocking, catching, and parrying), and counter-attacking. This exercise is an important exercise because it develops the specific hand and feet correlation needed for these various aspects of Muay Thai.

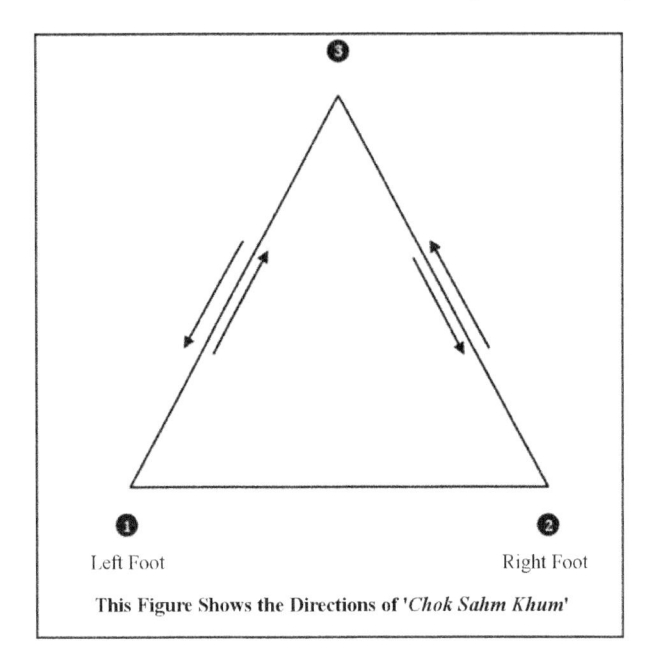

This Figure Shows the Directions of '*Chok Sahm Khum*'

(position 1: Left Foot; position 2: Right Foot; position 3: apex)

How to Do It: Look at the picture

The Ready Position

1. Stand shoulder width apart. Left foot at (1). Right foot at (2)

2. Lift your hands, your left fist touches the outside tip of your left eyebrow. Your right fist touches the outside tip of your right eyebrow. Tuck your arms to your body.

3. Step the left foot (1) to (3) with the feet moving close and parallel to the floor as you throw the left straight punch forward. When throwing the straight punch forward, your shoulders should narrow up in a straight line with the target. This is important because it trains you to be a smaller target.

4. When your left foot is at position (3), your left fist/hand hits the (imaginary target) - at the same time.

5. Your eyes look at the tip of your left fist. Your chin, tucks into the left shoulder and your right hand is stuck to the right eyebrow. Your right elbow stays tucked toward your body.

6. Pull the left foot from (3) back to (1), bringing your left fist back to touch your left eyebrow.

7. Step the right foot (2) to (3), with the feet moving close and parallel to the floor as you throw the right straight punch forward. When throwing the straight punch forward, your shoulders should narrow up in a straight line with the target. This is important because it trains you to be a smaller target.

8. When your right foot is at position (3), your right fist/hand hits the (imaginary target) - at the same time.

9. Your eyes look at the tip of your right fist. Your chin, tucks into the right shoulder and your left hand is stuck at the left eyebrow. Your left elbow stays tucked toward your body.

10. Pull the right foot from (3) back to (2), bringing your right fist back to touch your right eyebrow.

11. Repeat Steps 1-10 for 2-3 minutes.

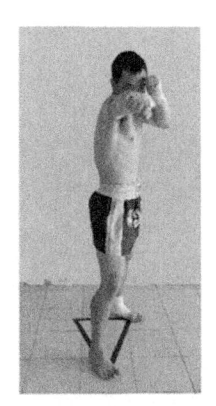

Technique: As you start out to practice this exercise, practice with open hands instead of a clenched fist to maximize the benefit of this exercise.

The benefit of this exercise 'Straight Punch forward from Square Stance' is that it teaches your body how to feel balanced throwing punches from both stances. It helps to correlate your hand movement with your feet movement in the way of moving which is specific to Muay Thai. In order to learn how to fight from both stances, you must feel equally comfortable moving and throwing your weapons from both sides. This footwork drill will help with that.

This is the beginning point of learning to fight equally on both sides. If you can do '*Chok Sahm Khum*' really well, learning your '*1/8 Turn In*' and '*1/4 Turn In*' footwork as well as the other footwork movements from both stances will also be a lot easier to learn.

Something to Remember: For this exercise, your hand starts at your eyebrows, are thrown from the eyebrow, and always return back to the eyebrow when the punch returns. The eyes must be at the end of the fist, at the knuckles of the index and middle finger. Your chin tucks to the shoulder of the arm throwing the punch. Elbow tucks to the body. The drill is not meant to be done quickly, but following this proper rhythm - When the punch lands, the foot lands, the same time.

Sharpening Your Step Forward Cross: (Exercise) The following exercise is used to sharpen how you step forward into your cross and another beginning exercise for learning to develop your rear hand punch from both your Orthodox and Southpaw Stances.

How to Do It (From the Orthodox Stance):

1. Start from standing in the Orthodox Stance.

2. Step with both feet, using your *Zig-Zag Footwork*(*'Yhang Salab Fun Bla'*) moving across of the centerline to throw the cross with the right hand. The right foot touches the floor the same time the right hand hits the (imaginary) target.

3. Step with both feet, using your *Zig-Zag Footwork* moving across the centerline to throw the cross with the left hand. The left foot touches the floor the same time the left hand hits the (imaginary) target.

4. Step using your *Zig-Zag Footwork* moving across the centerline to throw the cross with the right hand. The right foot touches the floor the same time the right hand hits the (imaginary) target.

Repeat steps 3 and 4 until you feel can throw the Cross, stepping forward, equally well from both sides.

Remarks:

1. When you throw your punches your fists and your feet need to move in good correlation. In other words, when stepping with your punches, the foot on the same side as the throwing arm touches the floor the same time the fist touches the target. That's when you maximize the weight of the punch.

2. You can use this exercise to practice your hooks, uppercuts, and elbows with *Zig-Zag Footwork* until you can deliver all of them with the same feeling and same amount of heaviness from both Orthodox and Southpaw Stances.

Technique: As you start out to practice this exercise, practice with open hands instead of a clenched fist to maximize the benefit of this exercise.

Sharpening Your Cross (Throwing in Place) (Exercise) The following exercise is used to sharpen your cross standing in place. It is another beginning exercise for learning to develop your rear hand punch from both your Orthodox and Southpaw Stances.

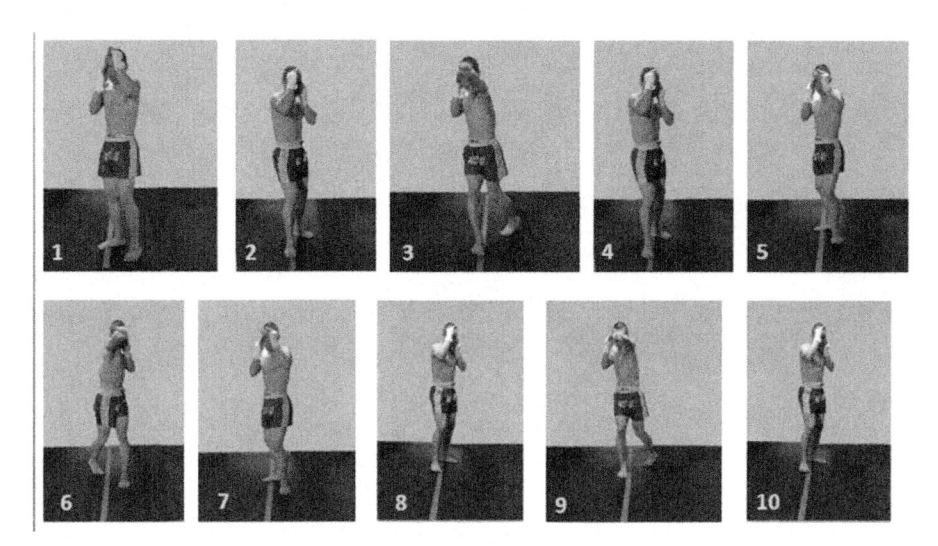

How to Do It (From the Orthodox Stance):

1. Start from standing in the Orthodox Stance.

2. *Switch Stance Back* into your Southpaw Stance.

3. Without stepping forward, throw the Southpaw Cross with your left hand, sending the force forward by using your left ball of the foot as the pivot point.

4. Twist your left ball of the foot back into stance to bring your left hand back to your face.

5. *Switch Stance Back* into your Orthodox Stance.

6. Without stepping forward, throw the Orthodox Cross with your right hand, sending the force forward by using your right ball of the foot as the pivot point.

7. Twist your right ball of the foot back into stance to bring your right hand back to your face.

8. *Switch Stance Back* into your Southpaw Stance.

9. Without stepping forward, throw the Southpaw Cross with your left hand, sending the force forward by using your left ball of the foot as the pivot point.

10. Twist your **left ball of the foot** back into stance to bring your **left hand** back to your face. Repeat Steps 5-10 until you feel you can throw the Cross, standing in place, equally well from both sides.

Chapter 15 - The Daily Training Routines of a Nak Muay

The Mental Strength of the Muay Thai Fighter

Inside of the ring, the boxer never gives up, doesn't show fear to the opponent, and doesn't show any pain or exhaustion during combat.

He trains and fights with an indomitable spirit, and at the end of the fight, win or lose, the result is the result.

When we as humans engage in hand to hand combat against one another, we follow our natural instincts such as fear, anger and courage. The physical and mental training routine of a Muay Thai fighter is meant to create new natural instincts of body movement for this particular kind of combat.

In order to develop these new instincts, the Nak Muay must train according to the time-tested basics of what it takes to be a Muay Thai fighter, regularly.

There are certain exercises that the Nak Muay executes as ritual daily to condition both mind and body for stepping into combat.

The Daily Warm-Up of the Muay Thai Fighter

1. **Aerobic Running / Sprinting** - The Nak Muay begins his training with running. The run includes moderate jogging interspersed with full out sprints for 10-15 seconds, similar to the pace of an intense exchange inside of the ring.

   It is important to always warm-up with walking or light jogging at the start of a run and get into a proper breathing rhythm.

2. **Jumping Rope** - Jumping rope teaches the Nak Muay to be light on their feet. It also develops the correlation between the feet and hands, which is necessary for executing all Muay Thai techniques efficiently.

3. **Wrapping the Hands** - The third exercise is hand wrapping. A Nak Muay wraps his hands to protect the wrist and pad the knuckles before engaging in training. The Nak Muay uses this time to clear the mind of outside priorities, and sets an intention for the training session.

4. **Perform the Wai Kru** - The Wai Kru is a set of ritualistic movements performed in order to pay homage to your Kru Muay. The Wai Kru may be different, depending on one's instructor. The intent is the same however, - to pay respect to your teacher.

Understanding the Wai Kru as a Foreigner

Muay Thai is a deep art, with a long history and culture. It's old and it might be hard for foreigners to understand why Thai fighters perform the Wai Kru. Similarly, it might be difficult for other religions to understand our concept of God and why certain religions give thanks before eating.

Every Trainee, every Muay Thai practitioner, if they have reached any level of skill, had been trained by some teacher. Even though you might not understand fully what the Wai Kru is about, it's part of the Muay Thai culture. If anything at least feel thankful for the information from your teacher. Feel gratitude. If you don't have gratitude your heart, your mind is not ready to learn.

Before Muay Thai became a sport with rules and regulations, fighters wouldn't necessarily fight inside of a ring with a standard floor surface. Sometimes the ground would be uneven and performing the Wai Kru would allow fighters to survey the ground and find their footing before the fight. Even today, between matches, some spots of ring are wet and you can survey those spots before the match and be careful not to slip at those areas during the fight.

The Wai Kru is a form of meditation, a warmup for the body, your final opportunity to center your body and mind before the fight. Once the referee says fight, you don't have that time anymore.

5. **Warm-Up Basic Techniques** - After performing the Wai Kru, the Nak Muay warms up the basic techniques of Muay Thai known as 'Mae Mai Muay Thai'. Some Kru Muay may have their students learn and sharpen their Mae Mai through the practice and refinement of basic Muay Thai Boran forms as part of their daily warm-up.

About the Daily Warm Up Exercises of the Muay Thai Fighter

Each of these warm-up exercises has a specific purpose of conditioning the body for what it takes to be a Muay Thai fighter - mentally, physically, and spiritually. Through adherence to these exercises as daily rituals, the body and mind develop a deep integration with the warrior spirit of the art.

The discipline of performing these exercises with unwavering and unflinching commitment, even on days where there is physical tiredness or simply lack of motivation, teaches the Nak Muay to overcome adversity, self-discipline, and the physical ability to overcome adversity.

The Mindset for Sharpening Your Muay Thai Weapons

To do this, the Nak Muay must think as he trains his weapons. The two questions that the Nak Muay's mind should be attuned to as he executes each technique of the form, striking only the air.

1. How am I intending to use this weapon?

2. How do I generate the most amount of power, utilizing the correct form?

Each Muay Thai technique can be thrown with the full weight of the body behind them, and the student must discover how to do and feel that through repetitive training. Repetitive sharpening of the same basic punches, kicks, knees, elbows is an on-going practice for the Nak Muay. This is a daily practice to ingrain these techniques deeper and deeper into the subconscious.

The training of a Nak Muay is comprised of 1- training the body for physical strength 2- training the body for speed, 3- controlling the mind, and 4- developing aptitude and sagacity with the art of Muay Thai.

Training the Body

In addition to training their physical bodies, Thai fighters eat foods that provide their bodies the energy it needs for the rigorous training they endure daily and support their body's recovery from training. Typical daily exercises in their training include

•Practicing and Drilling Footwork

- Shadowboxing (sometimes with 1 lbs. dumbbells on each hand)
- Punching a small hanging ball
- Bagwork
- Padwork
- Clinching
- Push-ups / Pull-ups / Ab work
- Running
- Jump Rope
- Swimming
- Meditation

Training the Mind and Emotions of a Fighter

Before you start to training Muay Thai, you need to be really determined to do it because throughout the training you are going to face huge obstacles. If you just want to learn it quickly, it won't happen. In training, there is always some sort of accident that happens especially when you train with other trainees or your trainers.

Most people get upset, but you as a Nak Muay need to control that feeling. You shouldn't feel upset at all just because that's the kind of person you are; NOT because you are trying not to feel upset. This sense of not being easily perturbed is critical in the ring. You never get angry in training sessions and in the ring. If you can't do that, you won't win.

When training, the Nak Muay needs to train his brain to think clearly about combat. Through training with his Kru, the Nak Muay learns the vast number of ways for responding to the actions of his opponent.

There are a vast, vast number of Muay Thai techniques, each used for a different situation. You must be able to think of the various ways you can respond to the opponent and quickly pick the best response. As you train your body instincts to defend, say the jab. What's a good action to take in this fighting scenario? What's better? What's best? Always be thinking in these terms about what the possibilities are about what to do next. The brain needs to think fast for Muay Thai!

Training for Muay Thai Aptitude

All of the basic Muay Thai weapons are executed from the stance, utilizing the proper footwork movements, and knowing the distance to the killing spots of your opponents' body.

Using your brain, eyes, and body, you develop a sense for the distance between you and your opponent so that you can throw the best possible weapon to the opponent with accuracy.

Training the Eyes to See Accurately

You must train your eyes need to see what kind of weapon is coming to you in a split second. This is critical because Muay Thai is not an exercise, but is an art of self-defense. Without seeing what's coming toward you, you can't defend yourself.

Professional Thai fighters in the old days trained their eyes by hitting on water surfaces, while trying not to blink when the water got into their eyes.

A simple practice for training the eyes is to let someone throw weapons at you (not really hitting you), then you train your eyes to see what's coming at you and imagine what you would do to defend yourself next.

For defending, the eyes remain fixed near the sternum, gazing through the opponent, allowing you to see not just any of the weapons the opponent can throw at you, but allow you to survey your surroundings as you move about.

When throwing a heavy shot, the eyes should be focused intently on the target you are trying to hit. The eyes should see the opening before the weapon is thrown. The eyes are used to track the weapon to the target. You must train your eyes to see this way as you shadowbox.

Training to Become a Fighter

First of all, you need to have the basics of Muay Thai knowledge and understanding. If you're impatient and train perfunctorily, you are not going to be a fighter. At the point of when you are considering to fight, your skill in the basics, or *'Mae Mai Muay Thai'*, must be legit.

Daily roadwork (a.k.a. – running) is a must if you are training to fight in the ring. Run everyday, plus track your gas tank by sprinting at the same distance, and see how you can reduce the time to sprint that distance. Record that high record as your new target to beat.

Fighters in Thailand typically train twice a day, five to six days a week – once in the AM, and again in the late afternoon, coupled with copious road work. Training includes heavy bag work, pad work, sparring and clinching with other fighters and trainers.

Chapter 16 - Before You Start Training Muay Thai

Before you start to train your body and mind to learn Muay Thai, one thing that you need to really understand first is about human instincts. When we as humans engage in physical hand-to-hand combat against another human being, we follow our natural instincts and our strong emotions (fear, anger, courage, etc.)

In a fight between two untrained persons, where natural instinct and strong emotions take over, it is likely that the winner is the one who has the most physical strength. However, the winner, strong as he is, still gets hurt by his opponent.

This kind of fighting indicates a lack of consciousness towards combat and both the winner and loser always end up damaged. The priority of the Muay Thai fighter is 1st – to not get hurt and 2nd to hurt someone else.

Training Muay Thai helps you to create new natural instincts in your body and mind. However you need to train hard to create these new instincts. It takes discipline, repetition, and passion in order to build and install a new habit into your nervous system, but the result is transformative, in body and mind. You will be surprised about who you become.

To train for new body instincts and habits is to revolutionize your body routines. For example, when we walk, the lead leg is opposite of the lead arm. But in Muay Thai, you need to train the lead leg and the lead arm to be on the same side while you are 'walking' with the Muay Thai footwork.

How to Create New Natural Instincts and Habits

Muay Thai is the Art of 8 Limbs. The weapons – what are they? They are your two hands, two feet, two knees, and two elbows. Now ask yourself, what can you do with them with just your natural instincts?

Take for example, your straight punch. How do you think you would be able to generate your entire body weight through that punch. Do you think it's even possible? You might have no clue at first, but that's okay. This is part of the training - Being ready to install new instincts and habits into your body. When you first start training, the training will always make you feel that you're doing something awkward, against your natural instincts.

How do we add power to your weapons? Well, it's going to be a long fun ride. All you have to do is keep repeating the movements that you feel go against your natural instincts, repeating them using your consciousness, doing it until it becomes part of your subconscious.

Using the Imagination when Shadowboxing

Imagination is important when shadowboxing. When practicing your 2-step, 3-step, and 4-step offensive combinations, keep sharpening your brain by thinking what "steps" and combinations could happen next between you and your opponent. By using your imagination in training, fighting against an imaginary opponent (who may or may not be fighting back at you), not only will you improve in skill faster, but you will learn to be more efficient with your energy because you won't just be punching and kicking blindly into the air.

Time to Walk

Each of the 19 footwork movements of Muay Thai described in this book has its' own purpose. The top goal of your footwork is always to position your body in an advantageous spot in relation to your opponent, always ready to defend.

To be able to 'walk' in Muay Thai, you need huge effort to overcome your natural body instincts. You must repeat every move until it becomes your subconscious. Remember, you are always putting yourself in the advantageous situation. Always. As you fight, you must feel – "I own this game".

Addendum

Additional Defensive Techniques

Listed below are some of the many defensive techniques of Muay Thai, categorized in the following way:

1. How to Defend using the Punch
2. How to Defend using the Kick
3. How to Defend using the Elbow
4. How to Defend using the Knee
5. Defend the Elbow by Catching and Breaking

How to Defend using the Punch

(Attacker and Defender both fighting from the Orthodox Stance)

1. Defend the Jab -with- Cross

Attacker: Throws the Jab to the face.

Defender: Step back with *Retreat* (at the same time the Attacker steps in to throw his Jab), using your left palm to scoop the attackers' Jab hand down and toward your belly. Then, throw your Cross to the attackers' **jaw**.

2. Defend the Right High Kick -with- Jab

Attacker: Step forward with your left foot and throw the right high kick to the defenders' neck.

Defender: *Step Forward* throwing the Jab to the attackers' **chin** (at the same time the Attacker steps in to throw his kick). Your left foot touches the floor the same time your left fist touches the Attackers' chin.

Remarks: Because the Muay Thai kick follows an arced trajectory to its target vs. the jab which follows a straight line to the target, if you throw the Jab at the same time the attacker throws the kick, the Jab will reach the target before the kick. The more you can step into the opponent's space with *Step Forward* to throw the jab when they kick, the safer you will be from the heaviness of the kick.

3. Defend the Left High Kick -with- Cross

Attacker: Step with the right foot and throw the left kick to the defenders' neck.

Defender: Use *Slant Step (left)* (at the same time the Attacker steps in to throw his Kick), to step just off the centerline away from the incoming kick while shooting a snappy cross to the attackers' **face**.

Trick: Your footwork, *Slant Step (left)* with the Cross must be executed in rhythm with the attackers' footwork for his kick.

4. Defend the Left Straight Knee –with- Right Short Uppercut

Attacker: Step with the right foot to throw left straight knee to the defenders' body.

Defender: Use *Slant Step (left)* (at the same time the Attacker steps in to throw his knee) to step just off the centerline away from the incoming force, dipping the hips slightly to be able to drive up on the Rear Short Uppercut to the attacker's **chin**.

Remarks: Imagine a straight line arrow from the Attackers' belly button pointing straight up to his chin. The uppercut maximizes its power when thrown along this trajectory to the target.

How to Defend using the Kick

(Attacker and Defender both fighting from the Orthodox Stance)

1. Defend the Jab –with- Left Body Kick

Attacker: Throws the Jab to the Defenders' Face.

Defender:

>Step 1: Use *Pivot Step (right)* (at the same time the Attacker steps in to throw his Jab) using your rear hand to parry the opponents left wrist down and away from you.
>
>Step 2: Step with the right foot and throw the Left Kick to the Attackers' **Ribs**

2. Defend Jab –with- Left Body Kick

Attacker: Throws the Jab to the defender's Face

Defender: Use *Slant Step (Right)* (at the same time the Attacker steps in to throw his Jab), shifting all of your weight onto your right foot to move off the centerline and the throw left kick to the attackers' **body**.

3. Defend Right Low Cut Kick –with- Right High Kick

Attacker: Step with the left Foot, dropping the body slightly to throw the right low cut kick to the outside part of the knee joint.

Defender: Absorbs the low kick and exchange it immediately by throwing the right high kick to the **head**, stealing the shot quickly before the opponent can return to his guard.

4. Defend Left Low Inside Cut Kick –with- Left High kick.

Attacker: Step with the right foot to throw the left cut kick to the inside of the defenders' lead knee joint.

Defender: Use *Switch Stance Back* to evade the kick. From your Southpaw stance, step forward with your right foot and throw the left kick to the attackers' **neck**.

5. Defend Right Low Cut Kick –with- Right High Kick

Attacker: Steps with the left foot and throws the right low kick to the outside part of the defenders' left knee joint

Defender: Use *Retreat* to evade the kick completely. Once the attackers' foot passes by the centerline, immediately step forward and throw the right kick to the **neck**.

How to Defend using the Elbows

(Attacker and Defender both fighting from the Orthodox Stance)

1. Defend Jab –with- Left Downward Hit Elbow or Left Cut Elbow.

Attacker: Throws the Jab to the defenders' face.

Defender: Use *1/4 Turn In (Left)* to evade the Jab to the inside angle and throw Left Downward Hit Elbow or Cut Elbow to the attacker's **face**.

Remarks: To send the driving force through the Downward Hit Elbow or Cut Elbow, pivot on the left ball of the foot.

2. Defend Jab –with- Left Spear Elbow

Attacker: Throws the Jab to the defenders' face.

Defender: Throw Spear Elbow to the **aorta** or **eyes**, using *1/8 Turn In (Left)*, ending with the body turned 45° from the centerline.

Remarks: To send the driving force through the Spear Elbow, your left foot touches the floor the same time your left elbow touches the target.

3. Defend Right Downward Hit Elbow –with- Right Up Elbow.

Attacker: *Step forward* and throw Right Downward Hit Elbow to the Defenders' face

Defender:

Step 1: Use *Slant Step (right)* and use your left elbow to block the Downward Hit Elbow. Left hand touches the left ear.

Step 2: Step toward the opponent with your left foot and throw right Up Elbow to the attackers' **chin**.

4. Defend Jab -with- Jumping Right Tomahawk Elbow

Attacker: *Step Forward* and throw the Jab to the defenders' Face

Defender:

Step 1: Use *Diagonal Retreat (right)* to evade the Jab with your footwork

Step 2: Step toward the attacker with the **left foot**, pushing off the **left foot** to jump and throw right Tomahawk Elbow to the attackers' **left shoulder**.

How to Defend using the Knees

(Attacker and Defender both fighting from the Orthodox Stance)

1. Defend Jab –with- Left Flare Knee

Attacker: Throws Jab to the defenders' Face.

Defender: Use *Slant Step (right)* to step off the centerline away from the jab and throw left Flare Knee to the attackers' **rib cage**, getting your two hands behind the opponents back and pulling the attacker into the left Flare Knee.

2. Defend Right Low Cut Kick –with- Right Cut Knee

Attacker: Step with left foot and throw right low cut kick to the defender's upper left leg

Defender: Turn your body by using your left ball of the foot as the pivot point and swing your right upper leg to hit the **upper leg** of the opponents' kicking leg with your folded knee.

Remarks: The part that lands on the target (opponent's upper leg) is the knee.

3. Defend the Left Body Kick –with– Right Straight Knee

Attacker: Step with right foot to throw the left kick to the defenders' lower rib cage.

Defender: Step with the left foot and throw the right straight knee or floating knee to the attackers' **belly**.

How to Defend the Elbow by Catching and Breaking

(Attacker and Defender both fighting from the Orthodox Stance)

Attacker: *Step forward* with left foot to throw right downward hit elbow to the opponents face.

Defender: Use *1/4 Turn Out (left)* to step away from the incoming force. As you turn your body for *1/4 Turn Out (left)*, use your right hand to catch the attackers' right wrist (the throwing arm) in the way that your right palm faces up. Simultaneously use your left hand to catch the attackers' right elbow with your palm faced down. As you complete *1/4 Turn Out (left),* pull both of your hands into your body as you turn the opponents' lower arm clockwise. This should all be done in one swooping motion. After catching and **breaking the elbow**, throw the right straight knee to the attackers' **body** or **face**.

Additional Offensive Combinations

As mentioned in Chapter 11 – The Art of Muay Thai Offense', offensive combinations are executed by combining your basic weapons ('*Mae Mai Muay Thai*') together, attacking with tricks and bluffs, as well as real attacks. 'Real' in the sense that you are really throwing with the weight of your body behind the strike with the intent to do damage. Normally, long range weapons that are thrown with snappiness and precision are used to 'open' for your offensive combinations. The strikes that follow the opening attack can be short distance or long distance, depending on the result of your opening weapon.

The combinations listed in this Addendum are Two-steps, Three-steps and Four-steps, Five-steps and Six-steps. When to use these combinations depends on the particular fighting situation. These combinations can be thrown at different rhythms, with all of the weapons in a combination thrown as all bluffs or all real, or a combination of fake and real. In order to do this, the fighter must have excellent skills in using their '*Mae Mai*'.

By switching the direction of your attack from step to step in your offensive combinations, you make the opponent more anxious about where they need to defend, making yourself a more difficult opponent to handle.

2-Step Combinations

1. Double Jab

2. Jab, followed by cross

3. Jab, followed by Lead Short Uppercut

4. Jab, followed by Rear Short Uppercut

5. Cross, followed by Lead Overhand

6. Cross to the belly, followed by Lead Overhand

7. Jab, followed by Lead cut elbow

8. Jab, followed by Lead Spear Elbow

9. Jab, followed by Lead Straight Knee

10. Jab, followed by Lead Kick

11. Jab, followed by Lead Teep

3-Step Combinations
1. Two Jabs, followed by cross
2. Jab, Lead Short Uppercut, Cross
3. Jab, Cross, Lead Overhand
4. Jab, Rear Short Uppercut, Lead Overhand
5. Jab, Kick, Cross
6. Jab, Cross, followed by Low Cut Kick
7. Jab, Rear Low Cut Kick, followed by Lead High Kick
8. Jab, Rear Teep, Lead Teep

4-Step Combinations
1. Jab, Cross to the Belly, Lead Overhand, Rear Low Kick
2. Jab, Lead Short Uppercut, Cross, Lead High Kick
3. Jab, Rear Short Uppercut, Lead Overhand, Rear Low Cut Kick
4. Jab, Lead Spear Elbow, Rear Up Elbow, Lead Cut Elbow
5. Jab, Rear Up Elbow, Lead Cut Elbow, Rear Downward Hit Elbow
6. Jab, Lead Spear Elbow, Rear Downward Hit Elbow, Lead Straight Knee

5- Step Combinations
1. Jab, Cross, Lead Overhand, Rear Low Kick, Lead High Kick
2. Jab, Lead Spear Elbow, Rear Up Elbow, Lead Cut Elbow, Rear Downward Hit Elbow
3. Jab, Rear Up Elbow, Lead Cut Elbow, Rear Downward Hit Elbow, Lead Straight Knee

6-Step Combinations
1. Jab, Lead Spear Elbow, Rear Up Elbow, Lead Cut Elbow, Rear Downward Hit Elbow, followed by Lead Straight Knee
2. Jab, Rear Up Elbow, Lead Cut Elbow, Rear Downward hit Elbow, Lead Straight knee followed by Rear High Kick

The Killing Spots of the Human Body

To execute your Muay Thai techniques more efficiently, you must understand the targets and the vulnerabilities of those targets – both on your opponent and on yourself.

Before being a competitive sport, Muay Thai Boran was used on the battlefield to defend the Kingdom of Siam. Many of the most effective techniques of Muay Thai target the killing spots to end an encounter fast and efficiently. The 'kill spots' are targets which if struck accurately and with sufficient force, render the opponent 1. unable to continue fighting or 2. potentially dead.

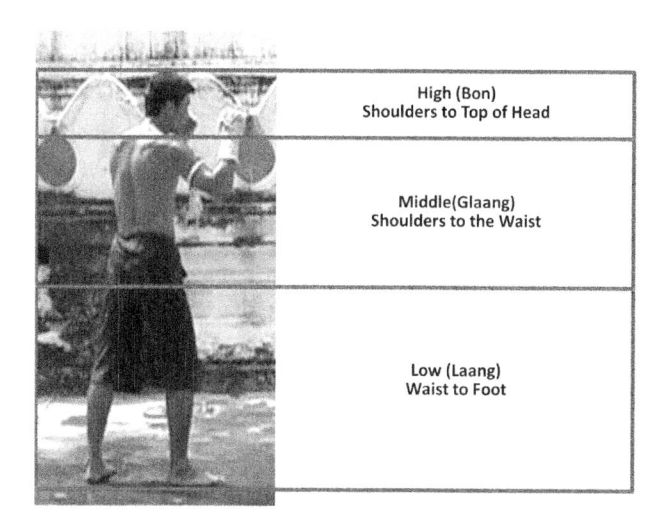

When discussing the targets of the body, Muay Thai teachers categorize the body into 3 levels – high, middle, and low.

3 Killing Spots Below the Waist

Understanding how to disable an opponent by targeting the legs is an effective strategy in a self-defense situation and a strategy the Nak Muay knows how to utilize as well as defend against.

1. The knee joint: If the knee joint is struck from the side, it can render an opponent immobile. The knee joint is a particular hinge joint which bears the weight of the body, and structurally weak in the horizontal direction.

Tears to the ligaments of the knee make it near impossible for the fighter to bear weight on the leg, immobilizing them from continuing to fight.

A common way of targeting the knee joint is by utilizing low cut kicks to the leg, which can be thrown to strike the inside of the Knee ('*Pawp Nai*') or to the outside of the knee ('*Pawp Nawk*').

The side teep can be delivered to the side of the knee as an opponent throws the high kick as demonstrated in the technique 'Ta-yae Kum Sao – Push Against a Pole, Diagonally'.

2. The Achilles Tendon is another 'Kill Spot' of the lower body. The Achilles Tendon is the largest tendon in the body. Trauma to this tendon, which has connections to muscles throughout the foot and leg, is very painful and a tear in this sensitive area can leave an opponent immobilized.

The straight kick is used to counter the straight teep by attacking the Achilles Tendon for the technique – ' Yuan Taud Hae – 'Tai Yuan Casting Net for Fish'.

3. The Groin - Although banned from use in competitive sport today, attacking the groin and genitals was also part of the arsenal of the Muay Boran warrior.

3 Killing Spots From the Waist to the Shoulders

1. The Floating Ribs - When attacking the torso with body kicks, the trajectory of the kick is diagonal *and* upwards into the lower ribs. The prime target of immobilization on the torso is the floating rib.

The floating ribs are the last two rows of the rib on the rib cage. Unlike the other 12 ribs, these ribs have no attachment to the anterior of the sternum like the other ribs, making them structurally very weak. The objective is to fracture or break these ribs.

To hit the floating rib, requires you to drive the shin up into the lower ribs.

Damage to this rib affects the *opponents'* ability to generate rotation through the spine without significant pain or breathe properly.

2. The Collar Bone (Clavicle) - Another killing spot on the torso is the clavicle. It is a brittle bone and can be broken with the flexed elbow joint.

For 'Hong Beek Hak – Break the Swans Wing', using your lead arm as a guard, step to the outside of your opponents' cross to break his clavicle, either using your Tomahawk Elbow or Downward Hit Elbow.

3. The Blood Vessels around the Heart - The area of the heart and chest are also considered 'killing spots'. Sufficient piercing trauma from a downward stabbing elbow such as the Tomahawk Elbow to the aorta, warriors from the past would aim to stop the heart with a technique such as 'Suk Puang Malai - Tattoo a Garland, on the Chest'.

*In Thailand, a 'Puang-Malai' (flower garland) tattooed on the chest, left of the heart, *is a common tattoo.*

4 Killing Spots from the Shoulders to the Head

There are 4 points above the shoulders which are considered killing spots for disabling an opponent (eyes) or knocking them unconscious (neck, chin, temple).

1. Artery on the Side of the Neck – There are major blood vessels which run along the side of the neck. Cutting off the blood flow to the head will create an instant knockout.

'Jarake Faht Haang - Crocodile Thrashes it's Tail' is used to defend yourself after a missed kick. As the opponent tries to capitalize off of your missed kick by stepping toward you to counter-attack, you throw the spinning back kick to his neck, pre-empting his counter-attack.

From the kick to the artery, the knockout occurs so quickly and definitively, that when opponents are struck by it, the knees buckle and the body drops dangerously to the ground, with the fall sometimes compounding the damage done.

2. The Pterion (commonly known as the temple) is the weakest part of the skull, where the major bones of the skull fuse together, and is rich with blood vessels and nerves. With sufficient impact from a *fist*, elbow strike, or kick, will cause the opponent to go unconscious.

3. The Chin, if struck, can cause instant knockout if hit with the correct timing. Knockouts coming from the opponent connecting with the chin result in a sharp transition to unconsciousness, also resulting in potential damage done from the fall.

4. The eyes are also a killing spot. Trauma to the eyes results in blurred vision or momentary blindness. Additionally, the ridges of the eyebrows are vulnerable to bleeding and cut open with punches and elbows. If placed with a stabbing type of elbow directly to the eye, can severely damage it and the areas around it. Damage to this area of the body can cause a loss of vision and places the injured in a very dangerous situation.

'Baksa-Waeg-Rung - Breaking into the Bird's Nest', one of the primary 'Mae Mai' Muay Thai techniques, involves merging into the opponents collarbone with *your Spear Elbow*.

By stepping *to the inner angle of the opponents guard, you pass his jab, 'breaking into the birdie's nest to land the Spear Elbow to the collar bone. The crossed hands create a heavier elbow while creating a defensive guard from the jab.*

'Baksa Waeg Rung' *can be used to target the eyes or the chin.*

Understanding the Killing Spots for your Fighting Style

By understanding the killing spots of your opponent and your fighting style which is going to be determined largely by your style of Muay, your body type, and your own personality, will dictate which techniques are more practical for you to utilize in a given combat scenario.

List of the 19 Footwork Movements of Muay Thai
(including Thai translations)

1. '**Step Forward**': (สืบหน้า) Thai Pronunciation: '*Sueb Na*'

2. '**Retreat**': (สืบหลัง) Thai Pronunciation: '**Sueb Laang**'

3. '**Switch Stance Forward**' (รุกสลับเท้า) Thai Pronunciation: '**Rook Salab-Tao**'

4. '**Switch Stance Back**' (ถอยสลับเท้า) Thai Pronunciation: '**Toi Salab-Tao**'

5. '**1/4 Turn Out (left)**' (ฉากนอกรุกซ้าย) Thai Pronunciation: '*Chawk Nawk Rook (Sai)*'

6. '**1/4 Turn Out (right)**' (ฉากนอกรุกขวา) Thai Pronunciation: '*Chawk Nawk Rook (Kwa)*'

7. '**Diagonal Retreat (left)**' (ฉากนอกรับซ้าย) Thai Pronunciation: '*Chawk Nawk Rup (Sai)*'

8. '**Diagonal Retreat (right)**' (ฉากนอกรับขวา) Thai Pronunciation: '*Chawk Nawk Rup (Kwa)*'

9a. '**1/8 Turn In (left)**' (ฉากในรุกซ้าย) Thai Pronunciation: '*Chawk Nai Rook (Sai)*'

9b. '**1/4 Turn In (left)**' (ฉากในรุกซ้าย) Thai Pronunciation: '*Chawk Nai Rook (Sai)*'

10a. '**1/8 Turn In (right)**' (ฉากในรุกขวา) Thai Pronunciation: '*Chawk Nai Rook (Kwa)*'

10b. '**1/4 Turn In (right)**' (ฉากในรุกขวา) Thai Pronunciation: '*Chawk Nai Rook (Kwa)*'

11. '**Pivot Step (left)**' (ฉากในรับซ้าย) Thai Pronunciation: '*Chawk Nai Rup (Sai)*'

12. '**Pivot Step (right)**' (ฉากในรับขวา) Thai Pronunciation: '*Chawk Nai Rup (Kwa)*'

13. '**Move Feet Around a Circle**' (การเคลื่อนเท้าเป็นวงกลม) Thai Pronunciation: '*Kluan Tao Wong Glom*'

14. '**Slant Step (left)**' (รุกเฉียงซ้าย) Thai Pronunciation: '*Rook Shiang (Sai)*'

15. '**Slant Step (right)**' (รุกเฉียงขวา) Thai Pronunciation: '*Rook Shiang (Kwa)*'

16. '**Zig-Zag Footwork**' (ย่างสลับฟันปลา) Thai Pronunciation: '**Yhang Salab Fun Bla**'

17. '**Parry Mid-line**' (ย่างสุขเกษม) Thai Pronunciation: '**Yhang SookaSem**'

18. '**Lift Knee**' (ย่างสูง) Thai Pronunciation '*Yhang Soong*'

19. '**Three Position Stepping**' (ย่างสามขุม) Thai Pronunciation: '*Yhang Sahm Khum*'

Epilogue

This book was specifically written for people interested in learning the art of Muay Thai. You may have just had your very first Muay Thai class today or have been practicing for several years. This book was written for you.

The purpose of the book is to share with you the profound knowledge I have gathered, studied, and researched from experiences studying under my instructor, Ajarn Sukchai of the Physical Education Institute of Lampang, Thailand, Kru Eric Karner of Nak Muay Gym, and the multitude of other fighters and friends I've met along the way across the world who've helped me along my own personal journey into learning the art.

What Lead to This Book Being Written

The year was 2007. After moving out from home in New Jersey after college, I started my engineering career at a large pharmaceutical company, as a deviation writer in PA. It was a great job and a great opportunity. Through that experience, I developed skills of communicating complex ideas through the written word.

At the time, my friends and I were into boxing and sparring with one another but never really formally trained in any martial art for an extended period of time.

After seeing a special on Muay Thai on a boring Saturday Night after a long week of 9-5 work, I connected immediately – "What is this Muay Thai stuff? – And how do I bring some of that into my life?"

The question that stirred in my head that night led me to meet Kru Eric Karner. Kru Eric took me under as a student, a fighter, and a friend. He taught me how to fight using the tools of Muay Thai and was always in my corner at my fights. Even more empowering, he taught me how to travel to Thailand on my own and travel across the country to expose myself to different fighters and trainers from around the world.

After my first trip, I was in love with all things Thai. And that love led me to meet my beautiful and loving wife, Poy. Through my Muay Thai journey, she's been with me and supported me through it all.

At some point, deep in my heart, I knew I wanted to transition from being a fighter to being a teacher. It's funny how when you align your heart and actions with what you desire that circumstances present themselves to you.

In 2012, my wife and I have our wedding ceremony in Thailand and I was accepted into the family as a son.

My Father-in-Law introduced me to Ajarn Sukchai, a College Professor of Muay Thai.

Ajarn Sukchai, a man in his mid-sixties had 38 years of teaching the art of Muay Thai. When I met him, he looked at me like a kid. He gave me an ultimatum – 'We train my way, or go train somewhere else."

And so I humbly decided that we should do things his way, and there in began my education into teaching Muay Thai.

Through training with Ajarn Sukchai, he taught me how to 'walk the like the Thai's' by learning the 19 basic footwork movements of Muay Thai.

He taught me how to categorize in my head the various types of punches, elbows, kicks, knees, and Teeps contained within the Muay Thai arsenal – and the appropriate time to use each of the weapons.

He taught how to use the multitude of combinations of footwork and weapons, and how to use them to counter any attack an opponent throws at me.

If I could sum it up - Ajarn Sukchai, taught me how to think about Muay Thai. He broke the game of Muay Thai down for me into such simple terms – that it became my own magnificent obsession of how to share it with the world outside of Thailand.

I would go to sleep with this question every night- How could I help speed up the learning process of those searching to unlock the power of Muay Thai for themselves?

And so this book is a distillation of the profound knowledge imparted upon me by Ajarn Sukchai, Kru Eric Karner, my wife, and everyone associated with this story, thus far. It was an effort, which used all of the qualities which I'm most proud of, drawing upon my experiences and skills as an engineer, writer, student, fighter, and instructor.

It is the book that I wish I had when I had first started training, and would have helped shaped the direction and vision who I could become through the practice of Muay Thai.

If you read this book, it will re-shape how you think about Muay Thai. It will break down the most important concepts a Muay Thai fighter needs to grasp to be successful – rhythm, brains, and footwork – and connects them to what's already out there about Muay Thai.

I want to thank you for taking the time to download this book. And as Ajarn Sukchai has said to me after one of our training sessions - "I have given you the knife – it's up to you to sharpen it."

About the Author

Anthony Yuan is the author of Muay Thai: The Footwork and has been a professional Muay Thai instructor for 8 years. Mr. Yuan received his purple pradjit under Kru Eric Karner and has competed 20+ Amateur Muay Thai Bouts both in the States and Thailand.

Since, 2008, Mr. Yuan has been travelling to Thailand annually to uncover the secrets of Muay Thai , training at gyms throughout Thailand. Mr. Yuan studied extensively as a student under Ajarn Sukchai at the Institute of Physical Education – Lampang, where he received his education in how to teach the Art of Muay Thai.

Mr. Yuan has graduated from Rutgers University in 2007 with a Bachelor's Degree in Biomedical Engineering and a Minor in Chemistry. He has always been an avid fitness enthusiast and a certified personal trainer.

He opened an currently operates Mastermind Muay Thai, in Kennett Square, serving the community by providing his instruction and teaching expertise locally at his school.

Printed in Great Britain
by Amazon